Taste of Home
Breads

T0044738

THIS BOOK IS GIVEN TO:

_____

WITH HEARTWARMING WISHES FROM:

_____

TASTE OF HOME BOOKS • RDA ENTHUSIAST BRANDS, LLC • MILWAUKEE, WI

Visit us at **tasteofhome.com** for other Taste of Home books and products.

ISBN:978-1-62145-696-4
LOCC: 2020945999

Executive Editor: Mark Hagen
Senior Art Director: Raeann Thompson
Editor: Hazel Wheaton
Assistant Art Director: Courtney Lovetere
Designer: Jazmin Delgado
Copy Editor: Ann Walter

Cover
Photographer: Jim Wieland
Set Stylist: Melissa Franco
Food Stylist: Megumi Garcia

Pictured on front cover:
Crusty Homemade
Cheddar Cheese Bread, p. 41
Pictured on back cover:
Brown Sugar Oat Muffins, p. 104;
Garlic Fontina Bread, p. 19;
Honey-Squash Dinner Rolls,
p. 53; Herb Biscuit Loaf, p. 164;
Caramel-Pecan Monkey Bread,
p. 205
Pictured on spine:
Cranberry Orange Walnut
Bread, p. 110

Printed in China
5 7 9 10 8 6

TABLE OF CONTENTS

More ways to connect with us:

SHOPTASTEOFHOME.COM

There's Something Special About Bread!

Among all the ways home cooks make their families feel cherished, there's something about homemade bread that sets it apart. Now cooks of all skill levels—from experienced bakers to those who have never opened a packet of yeast—can create the perfect loaf.

From the tantalizing aroma of a loaf of crusty bread fresh from the oven to beautifully wrapped quick breads given to friends and family as gifts, breads are a perfect way to spread the love. Homemade bread makes sandwiches something special, and handmade rolls elevate any dinner to a feast. Cinnamon rolls at breakfast make a rare treat, and that loaf of scrumptious banana bread—what could be better?

If you're looking for start-from-scratch recipes for homemade yeast breads and rolls, you'll find them here. A complete guide to the basics of bread making sets even novice bakers off on the right foot! And if you want quick and easy dinnertime solutions that make the most of supermarket shortcuts, they're here, too.

Quick breads both sweet and savory. Biscuits, scones and bagels. Breakfast rolls and muffins. Beautifully shaped braided loaves suitable for holiday tables. Tasty pull-apart creations that are fun for the whole family to make and eat...they're all here in the brand-new *Taste of Home Breads*!

Types of Bread

Yeast breads depend on a living organism for their height and texture. Yeast breads fall into two main categories: kneaded breads and batter breads.

- **Kneaded breads** are traditionally worked by hand to develop the gluten in the dough. Modern gadgets—a bread machine or a stand mixer fitted with a dough hook—take the work out of kneading, but the dough itself is still kneaded.

- **Batter breads** are beaten with a mixer to develop the gluten. These breads use less flour, so their dough is stickier than kneaded yeast breads. The finished breads have a coarser texture and a rugged, textured crust.

A **quick bread** gets its lift from a leavener such as baking soda or baking powder. The beauty of quick breads is right in their name—they're ready to pop in the oven and start baking right away rather than needing time to rise. In fact, most suffer in quality if not baked immediately after mixing.

YEAST BREAD INGREDIENTS

Ingredients and their particular qualities affect bread's texture, density and crust. Understanding the job of each ingredient will help you to understand the science of yeast breads.

Flours: Wheat flour contains an elastic protein called gluten, which is developed during kneading and gives bread its structure. Flours with high gluten content (hard flours), such as bread flour or all-purpose flour, yield the best results. Whole wheat and rye flours (soft flours) have less gluten; used alone, they make an extremely dense loaf. These flours are often used in combination with bread flour or all-purpose flour to achieve lighter, airier results.

Yeast: This microorganism consumes sugars in sweeteners and flours and produces carbon dioxide gas that stretches gluten strands to give breads a light, airy texture. Store yeast in the refrigerator or freezer.

Sweeteners are the food for yeast; they also tenderize, add flavor, promote browning and lengthen shelf life. White or brown sugar, molasses, honey and maple syrup are common sweeteners used in yeast breads.

Salt controls the yeast's growth. Use the amount given in the recipe—too much salt will prevent the yeast from growing, but not enough will let the yeast grow too fast too soon, and then collapse.

Liquids: Water and milk are the primary liquids used in bread. Water gives a crunchy crust; milk gives a softer crust and a more tender crumb. Always warm liquid to the temperature stated in the recipe. Too cold, and the yeast will be slow to activate; too hot, and it will kill the yeast.

Fats (and eggs) tenderize, add moisture, carry flavor and give richness to breads.

TYPES OF YEAST

Active dry yeast is the most commonly used type of yeast. It must be proofed before using *(right)* in order to activate the dormant organism. A standard packet of yeast contains approximately 2½ tsp. To use active dry yeast in recipes that call for instant yeast, increase yeast amount by 25%.

Instant and rapid-rise yeasts are finely granulated and cut the rising time for dough by up to half. They can be added directly to the dry ingredients and do not need proofing. Instant and rapid-rise yeast can be used interchangeably; rapid-rise yeast may contain dough conditioners, like ascorbic acid, to produce the quick rise. To use instant yeast in recipes that call for active dry yeast, use 25% less than the recipe calls for.

Bread machine yeast has fine, small granules that can be mixed easily into the dough. Like rapid-rise yeast, this type of yeast may contain dough conditioners.

Older cookbooks sometimes call for *cake yeast* (also known as fresh yeast or compressed yeast). Due to its short shelf life, it may be difficult to find—check the dairy case. Cake yeast is proofed at a lower temperature (80°-90°), and is most suitable for breads with a long, cool rise time.

There is type of yeast— *osmotolerant yeast*—designed for sugar-heavy doughs. It's also not as common as dry yeasts but is becoming more readily available. Look for it at your grocer or specialty food store.

Proofing Yeast

When we talk yeast breads, the term "proof" pops up in two ways: proofing yeast, and proofing dough. Proofing the dough comes after kneading (see p. 8).

Proofing yeast ensures that it is alive and ready to create carbon dioxide. Dissolve one ¼-oz. packet of active dry yeast in a dish with 1 tsp. sugar and ½ cup warm water (between 105° and 115°). Leave the mixture alone for 5 to 10 minutes to let the yeast do its work; when it starts to bubble and foam, you know it's alive and ready for bread.

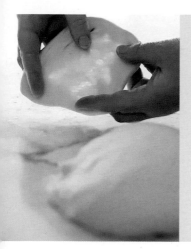

Kneading

Kneading helps develop gluten, which gives yeast bread its structure. (See instructions for kneading on p. 14.) To tell if you've kneaded the dough enough, look for two factors—smoothness and elasticity. To test the dough's elasticity, let it rest for about a minute and then press it with your finger. If the indentation stays, it's not yet ready. If the indentation springs back slightly, it's ready. If it springs back completely, it might be over-kneaded, and you may get tough, chewy bread. Finally, use the windowpane test. Tear off a piece of dough and stretch it between your fingers. If you can stretch it until you can see light through it when your hold it up, it's ready; if it tears, it needs more work.

PROOFING DOUGH

For the proofing (rising) stage, place the dough in greased bowl and cover it, then set the bowl in a warm (75° or above), humid and stable environment. Some options:

- Place a glass baking dish on your oven's bottom rack and fill it with boiling water; place your dough on the middle or top rack. Refresh the water every 30 to 45 minutes.

Some **oven lights** radiate enough heat for proofing even without turning on the heat. Turn on the light, then after about 30 minutes, use an oven thermometer to check the temperature; if the oven is 75°F or above, set your bowl of dough in the oven and shut the door, leaving the light on.

- Fill your **slow cooker** halfway with water and set it to the low setting. Put the lid on upside down, cover it with a dish towel, then set your bowl of dough on top.

Depending on temperature, humidity, the freshness of your yeast, and the type of dough, proofing can take from 1 to 3 hours. When ready, your dough should have expanded to roughly twice its original size and have a full, puffed appearance. To test the dough, gently poke it. It should feel soft and supple, and your finger should leave an indentation. Underproofed dough won't rise properly during baking.

If the dough looks stretched across the top and springs back instantly when pressed, it's overproofed, and may crack and collapse when baked. To fix overproofed dough, punch it down, knead it briefly and let it proof again until it's the correct size.

How Hard Do I Punch?

After proofing, you'll need to "punch down" the dough. The action isn't an actual fast punch—just press down firmly with your knuckles to remove some of the air.

REASONS YOUR BREAD ISN'T RISING

The little organisms that help your bread rise require extra care—warm temperatures, food and just-right conditions. If any of these variables are off, the dough may not rise the way it should. Here are some of the most common reasons your bread isn't getting the right lift.

1. The yeast is too old. To make sure your yeast is ready to go, be sure to proof it before adding to your dough.

2. The liquid is the wrong temperature. Too hot and the yeast will die; too cool and the yeast won't grow. Be sure that the liquid you use is between 105° and 115° F.

4. Too much salt. Salt controls the yeast so that it doesn't ferment too quickly—but too much salt can keep the yeast from doing its job. Measure carefully and never pour yeast and salt directly on top of one another in your mixing bowl.

5. Too much sugar. Sweet doughs take longer to rise because sugar absorbs the liquid in the dough so the yeast isn't as efficient. (Sweet doughs often proof overnight in the refrigerator). Measure carefully, don't add extra sugar, and allow cinnamon rolls and other sweet doughs plenty of time to rise.

6. Too much flour. Be mindful of your measurements and how much flour your dough picks up during kneading—too much can make the dough stiff and dry instead of slightly sticky and elastic. Use a bench scraper to scrape the dough off your work surface rather than being tempted to keep adding flour.

7. You're using whole grains. White flour creates wonderful gluten strands that give bread an airy texture, while whole wheat and other alternative flours don't develop gluten as easily or at all. Use a recipe specially formulated for those flours. If you want to add wheat flour into a recipe you already love, keep some all-purpose flour in the equation to help your bread rise.

8. The crust is too dry. The dough should be nice and moist; if a crust develops on top of the dough during proofing, it can be difficult for the bread to rise in the oven later. Cover your dough with a *damp* tea towel or plastic wrap while proofing. Spritz the plastic wrap with cooking spray to help keep it from sticking to the dough.

Baking at High Altitudes

At elevations above 3,000 feet, the lower air pressure makes the yeast rise more quickly—in as little as half the time. Keep an eye on your dough, and use about a third less yeast than called for in the recipe. Watch your flour content, too—add flour slowly, and don't add any more than absolutely necessary to make the dough manageable. It will also bake more quickly, too, so be sure to check for doneness a few minutes before the minimum baking time.

Bread-Making Tools & Equipment

It doesn't take a lot of gear or gadgets to get started bread baking. Here are some key tools and equipment for making the recipes in this book.

- Instant-read thermometer

- Stand mixer with paddle (for mixing) and dough hook (for kneading) attachments

- Rimmed baking sheet for baking rolls, scones, braided loaves and soda bread

- Wire cooling rack

- Bundt pan (for monkey breads and pull-aparts)

- Loaf pans: 8-in. and 9-in. For yeast breads, a smaller pan results in a tall loaf with a round top; you can use the larger pan for the same recipe and get a shorter loaf. Quick breads can call for either size or for mini loaf pans.

- Cast-iron skillet (for flatbreads and cornbreads)

- Rolling pin

- Bench scraper

- Muffin tins (standard, jumbo and mini sizes)

TIPS FOR USING A BREAD MACHINE

- Before you begin, carefully read your bread machine's manual.

- All liquid ingredients should be at room temperature (70° to 80°). This includes water, milk, yogurt, juice, cottage cheese, eggs and applesauce.

- Measure ingredients accurately and add in the order suggested by the bread machine manual.

- For best results, use bread flour and either active dry yeast or bread machine yeast. Bread machine yeast is finer, allowing for better dispersion during mixing and kneading. As a general guideline, for each cup of flour, use ¾ tsp. active dry yeast or ½ tsp. bread machine yeast.

- Check the dough after 5 minutes of mixing; it should feel smooth, soft and slightly tacky. If it's moist or sticky, add 1 Tbsp. flour and check again after a few more minutes of mixing. If it's dry and crumbly, add 1 Tbsp. liquid, then check again in 5 minutes.

- For food safety, recipes containing eggs, milk, sour cream, cottage cheese and other dairy or perishable foods should never be used on the delay-bake cycle.

CONVERTING RECIPES FOR BREAD MACHINES

Learning to convert traditional recipes for the bread machine requires experimentation. First, determine the size of your appliance. Look at the recipes that came with it. Note the amount of dry and liquid ingredients most of the recipes call for, and their proportion to sweeteners and fat.

Begin with a traditional bread recipe that has already given you good results. Once you successfully convert that for the bread machine, look for other recipes that use the amount of flour your machine required to make that recipe. Recipes for sourdough and refrigerated dough are not suitable for the bread machine.

For breads with toppings, filling or special shaping, just mix, knead and proof the dough in the bread machine. Punch dough down and finish shaping, rising and baking the traditional way.

Make notes about the conversion on the recipe for reference. If it wasn't quite right, adjust an ingredient and try again.

The chart below gives ingredient guidelines for bread machines yielding 1-lb., 1½-lb. and 2-lb. loaves.

INGREDIENT GUIDELINES FOR BREAD MACHINES

BREAD MACHINE SIZE	1 lb.	1½ lbs.	2 lbs.
FLOUR	2 to 2½ cups	3 to 3½ cups	4 to 4½ cups
LIQUID	⅔ cup	1 cup	1⅓ cups
ACTIVE DRY YEAST	1½ tsp.	2½ tsp.	3 tsp.
SUGAR	2 Tbsp.	3 Tbsp.	4 Tbsp.
SALT	1 tsp.	1½ tsp.	2 tsp.
FAT	4 tsp.	6 tsp.	8 tsp.

Storing Bread

One of the major advantages of homemade bread is also one of its potential drawbacks. Because it doesn't contain preservatives, it can be a race to finish a loaf before it goes stale. Homemade bread lasts 3-4 days when stored in a bread box. For long-term storage, freeze it—bread lasts for up 6 months in the freezer.

CHAPTER 1
Yeast Breads

Honey Bagels

Who has time to make from-scratch bagels? You do, with this easy recipe!
The chewy golden bagels offer a hint of honey and will win over even the pickiest eaters.
—Taste of Home *Test Kitchen*

PREP: 1 HOUR + STANDING • BAKE: 20 MIN. • MAKES: 1 DOZEN

1 Tbsp. active dry yeast
1¼ cups warm water
 (110° to 115°)
3 Tbsp. canola oil
3 Tbsp. sugar
3 Tbsp. plus ¼ cup honey,
 divided
1 tsp. brown sugar
1½ tsp. salt
1 large egg, room
 temperature
4 to 5 cups bread flour
1 Tbsp. dried minced
 onion
1 Tbsp. sesame seeds
1 Tbsp. poppy seeds

1. In a large bowl, dissolve yeast in warm water. Add the oil, sugar, 3 Tbsp. honey, brown sugar, salt and egg; mix well. Stir in enough flour to form a soft dough.

2. Turn onto a floured surface; knead until a smooth, firm dough forms, 8-10 minutes. Cover and let rest for 10 minutes.

3. Punch dough down. Shape into 12 balls. Push thumb through centers to form a 1½-in. hole. Stretch and shape dough to form an even ring. Place on a floured surface. Cover and let rest for 10 minutes; flatten bagels slightly.

4. In a large saucepan or Dutch oven, bring 8 cups water and the remaining honey to a boil. Drop bagels, 1 at a time, into boiling water. Cook bagels for 45 seconds; turn and cook 45 seconds longer. Remove bagels with a slotted spoon; drain and sprinkle with minced onion, sesame seeds and poppy seeds.

5. Place bagels 2 in. apart on baking sheets lined with parchment. Bake at 425° for 12 minutes. Turn and bake until golden brown, about 5 minutes longer.

1 BAGEL: 265 cal., 5g fat (1g sat. fat), 16mg chol., 303mg sod., 48g carb. (14g sugars, 2g fiber), 7g pro.

⊕

Stages of Working Yeast Bread

- **Kneading:** Fold the top of the dough toward you. With your palms, push dough with a rolling motion away from you. Turn dough a quarter turn; repeat folding, kneading and turning until the dough is smooth and elastic. Add a little flour to the surface as needed to avoid sticking.

- **Rising:** Cover dough with a clean towel and let rise in a warm (80°-85°), draft-free area. To check if the dough has doubled in size, press 2 fingers ½ in. into the dough. If the dents remain, the dough has doubled.

- **Punching down:** Press your fist quickly but gently into the center of the dough, then form it into a ball and knead 2-3 times. After punching down, let the dough rise a second time.

Basic Homemade Bread

If you'd like to learn how to make bread, here's a wonderful place to start. This easy bread recipe bakes up deliciously golden brown. There's nothing like the aroma wafting through my kitchen as it bakes.
—*Sandra Anderson, New York, NY*

PREP: 20 MIN. + RISING • **BAKE:** 30 MIN. • **MAKES:** 2 LOAVES (16 SLICES EACH)

1 pkg. (¼ oz.) active dry yeast
2¼ cups warm water (110° to 115°)
3 Tbsp. sugar plus ½ tsp. sugar
1 Tbsp. salt
2 Tbsp. canola oil
6¼ to 6¾ cups bread flour

1. In a large bowl, dissolve yeast and ½ tsp. sugar in warm water; let stand until bubbles form on surface. Whisk together the remaining 3 Tbsp. sugar, salt and 3 cups flour. Stir oil into yeast mixture; pour into flour mixture and beat until smooth. Stir in enough of the remaining flour, ½ cup at a time, to form a soft dough.

2. Turn dough onto a floured surface; knead until smooth and elastic, 8-10 minutes. Place in a greased bowl, turning once to grease the top. Cover and let rise in a warm place until doubled, 1½-2 hours.

3. Punch dough down. Turn onto a lightly floured surface; divide dough in half. Shape each into a loaf. Place in 2 greased 9x5-in. loaf pans. Cover and let rise until doubled, 1-1½ hours.

4. Bake at 375° until golden brown and bread sounds hollow when tapped or has reached an internal temperature of 200°, 30-35 minutes. Remove from pans to wire racks to cool.

1 SLICE: 102 cal., 1g fat (0 sat. fat), 0 chol., 222mg sod., 20g carb. (1g sugars, 1g fiber), 3g pro.

Garlic Fontina Bread

With its golden brown color and soft texture, this bread is a must at any family meal.
It's a modified version of a traditional white bread recipe my brother gave me.
Try it as garlic bread toast, for grilled sandwiches or enjoy as is.

—Cindy Ryan, St. Johns, MI

PREP: 30 MIN. + RISING • **BAKE:** 30 MIN. • **MAKES:** 2 LOAVES (16 SLICES EACH)

2 pkg. (¼ oz. each) active
 dry yeast
2 cups warm water
 (110° to 115°)
3 Tbsp. sugar
2 Tbsp. shortening
1 Tbsp. garlic powder
2 tsp. salt
5 to 5½ cups all-purpose
 flour
1½ cups plus 2 Tbsp.
 shredded fontina
 cheese, divided
1½ tsp. canola oil

1. In a large bowl, dissolve yeast in warm water. Add the sugar, shortening, garlic powder, salt and 3 cups flour. Beat until smooth. Stir in enough of the remaining flour to form a firm dough. Stir in 1½ cups cheese.

2. Turn dough onto a floured surface; knead until smooth and elastic, 6-8 minutes. Place in a greased bowl, turning once to grease the top. Cover and let rise in a warm place until doubled, about 1 hour.

3. Punch dough down. Shape dough into 2 loaves. Place in 2 greased 9x5-in. loaf pans. Cover and let rise in a warm place until doubled, about 30 minutes.

4. Preheat oven to 375°. Brush loaves with oil and sprinkle with remaining cheese. Bake for 30-35 minutes or until golden brown. Cool on a wire rack.

1 SLICE: 119 cal., 4g fat (2g sat. fat), 10mg chol., 215mg sod., 17g carb. (2g sugars, 1g fiber), 4g pro.

Perfect Pizza Crust

I have spent years trying different recipes and techniques, looking for the perfect pizza crust recipe—and this is it! I'm amazed that I finally found a crust recipe my family prefers over the pizza parlor's!

—*Lesli Dustin, Nibley, UT*

PREP: 20 MIN. + RISING • **BAKE:** 20 MIN. • **MAKES:** 8 SERVINGS

1   **Tbsp. active dry yeast**
1½ **cups warm water (110° to 115°)**
2   **Tbsp. sugar**
½   **tsp. salt**
2   **cups bread flour**
1½ **cups whole wheat flour**
   Cornmeal
   Pizza toppings of your choice

FLAVOR BRAVO!

This crust is fabulous as is, but you can add an extra burst of flavor by mixing a little garlic powder or dried herbs, like basil, rosemary, oregano or marjoram, in with the flour.

1. In a large bowl, dissolve yeast in warm water. Add the sugar, salt, 1 cup bread flour and the whole wheat flour. Beat until smooth. Stir in enough of the remaining bread flour to form a soft dough (dough will be sticky).

2. Turn dough onto a floured surface; knead until smooth and elastic, 6-8 minutes. Place in a greased bowl, turning once to grease the top. Cover and let rise in a warm place until doubled, about 1 hour.

3. Punch dough down; roll into a 15-in. circle. Grease a 14-in. pizza pan and sprinkle with cornmeal. Transfer dough to prepared pan; build up edges slightly. Add toppings of your choice.

4. Bake at 425° for 20-25 minutes or until the crust is golden brown and toppings are lightly browned and heated through.

1 SLICE (CALCULATED WITHOUT TOPPINGS): 193 cal., 0 fat (0 sat. fat), 0 chol., 149mg sod., 42g carb. (3g sugars, 4g fiber), 8g pro.

Traditional Hot Cross Buns

On Easter morning, our family always looked forward to a breakfast of dyed hard-boiled eggs and Mom's hot cross buns. I still serve these for special brunches or buffets.
—Barbara Jean Lull, Fullerton, CA

PREP: 25 MIN. + RISING • **BAKE:** 15 MIN. • **MAKES:** 2½ DOZEN

2 pkg. (¼ oz. each) active dry yeast
2 cups warm whole milk (110° to 115°)
2 large eggs, room temperature
⅓ cup butter, softened
¼ cup sugar
1½ tsp. salt
1 tsp. ground cinnamon
¼ tsp. ground allspice
6 to 7 cups all-purpose flour
½ cup dried currants
½ cup raisins
1 large egg yolk
2 Tbsp. water

ICING
1½ cups confectioners' sugar
4 to 6 tsp. whole milk

1. In a small bowl, dissolve yeast in warm milk. In a large bowl, combine eggs, butter, sugar, salt, spices, yeast mixture and 3 cups flour; beat on medium speed until smooth. Stir in currants, raisins and enough remaining flour to form a soft dough (dough will be sticky).

2. Turn dough onto a floured surface; knead until smooth and elastic, 6-8 minutes. Place in a greased bowl, turning once to grease the top. Cover and let rise in a warm place until doubled, about 1 hour.

3. Punch down dough. Turn onto a lightly floured surface; divide and shape into 30 balls. Place 2 in. apart on greased baking sheets. Cover with kitchen towels; let dough rise in a warm place until doubled, 30-45 minutes. .

4. Preheat oven to 375°. Using a sharp knife, cut a cross on the top of each bun. In a small bowl, whisk egg yolk and water; brush over tops. Bake 15-20 minutes or until golden brown. Remove from pans to wire racks to cool slightly.

5. For icing, in a small bowl, mix confectioners' sugar and enough milk to reach desired consistency. Pipe a cross on top of each bun. Serve warm.

1 BUN: 171 cal., 3g fat (2g sat. fat), 28mg chol., 145mg sod., 31g carb. (12g sugars, 1g fiber), 4g pro.

Chocolate Yeast Bread

Your family will love this tender loaf of chocolate bread. Slices are excellent when toasted and spread with butter, cream cheese or peanut butter.
—*Laura Cryts, Derry, NH*

4½ cups all-purpose flour
⅓ cup baking cocoa
2 Tbsp. sugar
1 pkg. (¼ oz.) active dry yeast
1 tsp. salt
¼ tsp. baking soda
1 cup water
½ cup 2% milk
½ cup semisweet chocolate chips
2 Tbsp. butter
1 large egg, room temperature
Optional: Baking cocoa and/or confectioners' sugar

1. In a bowl, combine 1¼ cups flour, the cocoa, sugar, yeast, salt and baking soda. In a saucepan, heat the water, milk, chocolate chips and butter; stir until chocolate is melted. Cool to 120°-130°. Add to dry ingredients; beat on medium speed for 2 minutes. Add ½ cup flour and egg; beat on high for 2 minutes. Stir in enough remaining flour to form a stiff dough.

2. Turn onto a floured surface; knead until smooth and elastic, 6-8 minutes. Place in a greased bowl, turning once to grease top. Cover and let rise in a warm place until doubled, about 1 hour.

3. Punch dough down. Turn onto a lightly floured surface; divide in half. Shape into loaves. Place in 2 greased 8x4-in. loaf pans. Cover and let rise until doubled, about 1 hour.

4. Bake at 375° until browned, 25-30 minutes. Remove from pans to cool on wire racks. Dust with baking cocoa and/or confectioners' sugar if desired.

1 SLICE: 124 cal., 3g fat (1g sat. fat), 11mg chol., 125mg sod., 22g carb. (3g sugars, 1g fiber), 3g pro.

Cardamom Braids

This is an old recipe that I like to make for breakfast.
The bread is great for dunking in a cup of coffee.
—*Walter Dust, Rapid City, MI*

PREP: 25 MIN. + RISING • **BAKE:** 25 MIN. • **MAKES:** 2 LOAVES (16 SLICES EACH)

1 pkg. (¼ oz.) active
 dry yeast
1½ cups warm 2% milk
 (110° to 115°), divided
1 cup sugar, divided
3 large eggs yolks, room
 temperature, lightly
 beaten
½ cup butter, softened
1 Tbsp. ground
 cardamom
½ tsp. salt
5 to 6 cups all-purpose
 flour
2 Tbsp. 2% milk

1. In a large bowl, dissolve yeast in ½ cup warm milk. Add ¾ cup sugar, egg yolks, butter, cardamom, salt, 3 cups of flour and the remaining warm milk; beat until smooth. Stir in enough of the remaining flour to form a soft dough.

2. Turn onto a floured surface; knead until smooth and elastic, 6-8 minutes. Place in a greased bowl, turning once to grease top. Cover and let rise in a warm place until doubled, about 1¼ hours.

3. Punch dough down; divide into 6 pieces. Shape each piece into a 16-in. rope. Place 3 ropes on a greased baking sheet; braid. Pinch ends firmly and tuck under. Repeat with the remaining 3 ropes on another baking sheet. Cover and let rise until doubled, about 45 minutes.

4. Brush braids with milk and sprinkle with remaining sugar. Bake at 350° until golden brown, 25-30 minutes. Remove to wire racks to cool.

1 SLICE: 135 cal., 4g fat (2g sat. fat), 29mg chol., 73mg sod., 22g carb. (7g sugars, 1g fiber), 3g pro.

Rustic Cranberry & Orange Bread

Studded with bright red cranberries and with a hint of orange flavor, slices of this pretty bread make the perfect holiday brunch treat.
—*Megumi Garcia, Milwaukee, WI*

PREP: 25 MIN. + CHILLING · **BAKE:** 50 MIN. · **MAKES:** 1 LOAF (16 SLICES)

1½ tsp. active dry yeast
1¾ cups water (70° to 75°)
3½ cups plus 1 Tbsp. all-purpose flour, divided
2 tsp. salt
1 Tbsp. cornmeal or additional flour
1 cup dried cranberries
4 tsp. grated orange zest

NOTES

1. In a small bowl, dissolve yeast in water. In a large bowl, mix 3½ cups flour and salt. Using a rubber spatula, stir in yeast mixture to form a soft, sticky dough. Do not knead. Cover; let rise at room temperature 1 hour.

2. Punch down dough. Turn onto a lightly floured surface. Pat into a 9-in. square. Fold the dough into thirds, forming a 9x3-in. rectangle. Fold the rectangle into thirds, forming a 3-in. square. Turn dough over; place in a greased bowl, turning once to grease top. Cover; let dough rise at room temperature until almost doubled, about 1 hour.

3. Punch down dough and repeat folding process. Return dough to bowl; refrigerate, covered, overnight.

4. Dust the bottom of a disposable foil roasting pan with cornmeal. Turn dough onto a floured surface; knead in the cranberries and orange zest. Shape into a 6-in. round loaf. Place in prepared pan; dust top with remaining 1 Tbsp. flour. Cover pan; let rise at room temperature until dough expands to a 7½-in. loaf, about 1¼ hours.

5. Preheat oven to 500°. Using a sharp knife, make a slash (¼ in. deep) across top of loaf. Cover pan tightly with foil. Bake on lowest oven rack 25 minutes.

6. Reduce oven setting to 450°. Remove foil; bake until deep golden brown, 25-30 minutes longer. Remove loaf to a wire rack to cool.

1 SLICE: 129 cal., 0 fat (0 sat. fat), 0 chol., 296mg sod., 28g carb. (5g sugars, 1g fiber), 3g pro.

Sourdough Starter

Some 25 years ago, I received some starter from a good friend. Here's how to make your own. The flavor will become more complex as you keep replenishing your starter.
—*Delila George, Junction City, OR*

PREP: 10 MIN. + STANDING • **MAKES:** ABOUT 3 CUPS

2 cups all-purpose flour
1 pkg. (¼ oz.) active dry yeast
2 cups warm water (110° to 115°)

1. In a covered 4-qt. glass, ceramic or plastic container, mix flour and yeast. Gradually stir in warm water until smooth. Cover loosely with a kitchen towel; let stand in a warm place 2-4 days or until mixture is bubbly and sour-smelling, with a clear liquid on top (pictured center left). Starter may darken, but if it turns another color or develops an offensive odor or mold, discard it and start over.

2. Cover tightly and refrigerate starter until ready to use. Either use and replenish starter or nourish it once every 1-2 weeks.

USE AND REPLENISH STARTER: Stir to blend in any liquid on top (pictured bottom left). Remove the amount of starter needed for your recipe; bring to room temperature before using. For each ½ cup starter removed, add ½ cup flour and ½ cup warm water to the remaining starter and stir until smooth. Cover loosely and let stand in a warm place 1-2 days or until light and bubbly. Stir; cover tightly and refrigerate.

TO NOURISH STARTER: Remove half of the starter. Stir in equal parts flour and warm water; cover loosely and let starter stand in a warm place for 1-2 days or until light and bubbly. Stir; cover tightly and refrigerate.

1 TBSP.: 19 cal., 0 fat (0 sat. fat), 0 chol., 0 sod., 4g carb. (0 sugars, 0 fiber), 1g pro.

Sage & Gruyere Sourdough Bread

A sourdough starter gives loaves extra flavor and helps the rising process. This bread, with sage and Gruyere cheese, comes out so well that I'm thrilled to share it.
—*Debra Kramer, Boca Raton, FL*

PREP: 35 MIN. + RISING • **BAKE:** 25 MIN. • **MAKES:** 1 LOAF (16 SLICES)

½ cup **SOURDOUGH STARTER** (p. 26)
1⅛ tsp. active dry yeast
⅓ cup warm water (110° to 115°)
½ cup canned pumpkin
½ cup shredded Gruyere cheese, divided
4 tsp. butter, softened
1 Tbsp. sugar
1 Tbsp. minced fresh sage
1 tsp. salt
2¼ to 2¾ cups all-purpose flour
1 large egg, lightly beaten

1. Let Sourdough Starter come to room temperature before using.

2. In a small bowl, dissolve yeast in warm water. In a large bowl, combine Sourdough Starter, pumpkin, ¼ cup cheese, butter, sugar, sage, salt, the yeast mixture and 1 cup flour; beat on medium speed until smooth. Stir in enough of the remaining flour to form a stiff dough (dough will be slightly sticky).

3. Turn onto a floured surface; knead until smooth and elastic, 6-8 minutes. Place in a greased bowl, turning once to grease the top. Cover and let rise in a warm place until doubled, about 1 hour.

4. Punch down dough. Turn onto a lightly floured surface; shape into a round loaf. Place on a greased baking sheet. Cover with a kitchen towel; let rise in a warm place until doubled, about 30 minutes. Preheat oven to 375°.

5. Brush egg over loaf; sprinkle with remaining cheese. Bake 25-30 minutes or until golden brown. Remove from pan to a wire rack to cool.

1 SLICE: 98 cal., 3g fat (1g sat. fat), 18mg chol., 186mg sod., 15g carb. (1g sugars, 1g fiber), 3g pro.

Roasted Red Pepper Bread

These savory loaves are moist, tender and loaded with flavor from grated Parmesan cheese and roasted sweet red peppers. They're great at dinner or as an appetizer.

—Cheryl Perry, Hertford, NC

PREP: 45 MIN. + RISING • **BAKE:** 20 MIN. • **MAKES:** 2 LOAVES (12 SLICES EACH)

1½ cups roasted sweet red peppers, drained
1 pkg. (¼ oz.) active dry yeast
2 Tbsp. warm water (110° to 115°)
1¼ cups grated Parmesan cheese, divided
⅓ cup warm 2% milk (110° to 115°)
2 Tbsp. butter, softened
1¼ tsp. salt
3¼ to 3¾ cups all-purpose flour
1 large egg
1 Tbsp. water
1½ tsp. coarsely ground pepper

1. Place red peppers in a food processor; cover and process until pureed. In a large bowl, dissolve yeast in warm water. Add the red peppers, 1 cup cheese, the milk, butter, salt and 1½ cups flour. Beat until smooth. Stir in enough remaining flour to form a firm dough.

2. Turn dough onto a floured surface; knead until smooth and elastic, 6-8 minutes. Place in a greased bowl, turning once to grease the top. Cover and let rise in a warm place until doubled, about 1 hour.

3. Punch dough down. Turn onto a lightly floured surface; divide dough into 6 pieces. Shape each into a 18-in. rope. Place 3 ropes on a greased baking sheet and braid; pinch ends to seal and tuck under. Repeat with remaining dough. Cover and let rise until doubled, about 1 hour.

4. In a small bowl, combine egg and water; brush over braids. Sprinkle with pepper and remaining cheese. Bake at 350° for 18-22 minutes or until golden brown.

1 SLICE: 99 cal., 3g fat (1g sat. fat), 15mg chol., 254mg sod., 14g carb. (1g sugars, 1g fiber), 4g pro. **DIABETIC EXCHANGES:** 1 starch.

Caraway Seed Rye Bread

My parents were immigrants from Czechoslovakia and my mother would pull out this rye bread recipe when guests came over for dinner. Every time I bake it, I get nostalgic for those days.
—*Millie Feather, Baroda, MI*

PREP: 20 MIN. + RISING • **BAKE:** 25 MIN. • **MAKES:** 2 LOAVES (10 SLICES EACH)

2 **pkg. (¼ oz. each) active dry yeast**
2 **cups warm water (110° to 115°), divided**
¼ **cup packed brown sugar**
1 **Tbsp. caraway seeds**
1 **Tbsp. canola oil**
2 **tsp. salt**
2½ **cups rye flour**
2¾ **to 3¼ cups all-purpose flour, divided**

1. In a large bowl, dissolve yeast in ½ cup warm water. Add the brown sugar, caraway seeds, oil, salt and remaining water; mix well. Stir in rye flour and 1 cup all-purpose flour; beat until smooth. Add enough remaining all-purpose flour to form a soft dough.

2. Turn dough onto a floured surface; knead until smooth and elastic, 6-8 minutes. Place in a greased bowl, turning once to grease top. Cover and let rise in a warm place until doubled, about 1 hour.

3. Punch dough down; divide in half. Shape each half into a ball; place in 2 greased 8-in. round baking pans or ovenproof skillets. Flatten balls to a 6-in. diameter. Cover and let rise until nearly doubled, about 30 minutes.

4. Bake at 375° for 25-30 minutes or until golden brown.

1 SLICE: 126 cal., 1g fat (0 sat. fat), 0 chol., 238mg sod., 26g carb. (4g sugars, 3g fiber), 3g pro.

No-Knead Honey Oatmeal Bread

We especially enjoy this tasty bread because we like using honey as a natural sweetener. We use the bread for both toast and sandwiches. It's lovely for special occasions, too.
—Janice Dancer, Williamstown, VT

PREP: 25 MIN. + RISING • **BAKE:** 40 MIN. • **MAKES:** 2 LOAVES (12 SLICES EACH)

2 cups water, divided
1 cup rolled oats
⅓ cup butter, softened
⅓ cup honey
1 Tbsp. salt
2 pkg. (¼ oz. each) active dry yeast
1 large egg, room temperature
4 to 5 cups all-purpose flour
Melted butter, optional

READER REVIEW
"I love this bread! I substituted 8 tsp. of applesauce for the butter to keep the healthy theme going and it turned out great. I will be making this instead of buying store-bought bread."
—TIFFANYLITTLE, TASTEOFHOME.COM

1. In a small saucepan, heat 1 cup water to boiling. Stir in the oats, butter, honey and salt. Let stand until mixture cools to 110°-115°, stirring occasionally. Heat remaining water to 110°-115°.

2. In a large bowl, dissolve yeast in the warm water. Add egg, the oat mixture and 2 cups flour. Beat until smooth. Stir in enough of the remaining flour to form a soft dough (dough will be sticky). Do not knead. Place in a greased bowl, turning once to grease the top; cover and let rise in a warm place until doubled, about 1 hour.

3. Punch down dough; divide evenly between 2 greased 8x4-in. loaf pans. Smooth tops of loaves. Cover and let rise in a warm place until doubled, 35-40 minutes. Using a sharp knife, make a shallow slash down the center of each loaf.

4. Bake at 375° until golden brown, 40-45 minutes. Remove from pans to wire racks to cool. If desired, brush with melted butter.

1 SLICE: 132 cal., 3g fat (2g sat. fat), 16mg chol., 325mg sod., 22g carb. (4g sugars, 1g fiber), 3g pro. **DIABETIC EXCHANGES:** 1 starch.

Apple Raisin Bread

I've been making this bread for many years. It smells so good in the oven and tastes even better. I make bread almost every Saturday, and it doesn't stay around long when our sons are home from college in the summer.
—*Perlene Hoekema, Lynden, WA*

PREP: 25 MIN. + RISING • **BAKE:** 30 MIN. • **MAKES:** 3 LOAVES (16 SLICES EACH)

- 2 **pkg. (¼ oz. each) active dry yeast**
- 1½ **cups warm water (110° to 115°), divided**
- 1 **tsp. sugar**
- 3 **large eggs, room temperature, beaten**
- 1 **cup applesauce**
- ½ **cup honey**
- ½ **cup canola oil**
- 2 **tsp. salt**
- 8 **to 9 cups all-purpose flour**
- 1½ **cups diced peeled apples**
- 1½ **cups raisins**
- 2 **Tbsp. lemon juice**
- 2 **Tbsp. cornmeal**

GLAZE
- 1 **large egg, beaten**
  Sugar

1. In a small bowl, combine the yeast, ½ cup water and the sugar; set aside. In a large bowl, combine the eggs, applesauce, honey, oil, salt and remaining water; mix well. Stir in yeast mixture. Gradually add enough flour to form a soft dough. Knead on a floured surface until smooth and elastic, about 10 minutes. Place dough in a greased bowl, turning once to grease top. Cover and let rise in a warm place until doubled, about 1 hour.

2. Punch dough down and turn it over in the bowl. Cover and let rise 30 minutes.

3. In a small bowl, combine the apples, raisins and lemon juice. Divide dough into 3 parts; knead a third of the apple mixture into each part. Shape each portion into a round, flat ball. Place each in a greased 8-in. round baking pan that has been sprinkled with cornmeal. Cover and let rise until doubled, about 1 hour.

4. Brush each loaf with egg and sprinkle with sugar. Bake at 350° for 30-35 minutes or until bread sounds hollow when tapped.

1 SLICE: 135 cal., 3g fat (0 sat. fat), 18mg chol., 105mg sod., 25g carb. (8g sugars, 1g fiber), 3g pro.

Homemade English Muffin Bread

Most of my cooking and baking is from scratch—I think it's worth the time and effort. Everyone enjoys homemade goodies like this delicious bread.
—Elsie Trippett, Jackson, MI

PREP: 20 MIN. + RISING • **BAKE:** 35 MIN. • **MAKES:** 2 LOAVES

5 cups all-purpose flour, divided
2 pkg. (¼ oz. each) active dry yeast
1 Tbsp. sugar
2 tsp. salt
¼ tsp. baking soda
2 cups warm 2% milk (110° to 115°)
½ cup warm water (120° to 130°)
Cornmeal

1. In a large bowl, combine 2 cups flour, the yeast, sugar, salt and baking soda. Add warm milk and water; beat on low speed 30 seconds, scraping bowl occasionally. Beat on high 3 minutes. Stir in the remaining flour (batter will be stiff). Do not knead.

2. Grease two 8x4-in. loaf pans. Sprinkle the pans with cornmeal. Spoon batter into pans and sprinkle cornmeal on top. Cover and let rise in a warm place until doubled, about 45 minutes.

3. Preheat oven to 375°. Bake 35 minutes or until golden brown. Remove from pans to wire racks to cool.

1 SLICE: 83 cal., 1g fat (0 sat. fat), 2mg chol., 165mg sod., 16g carb. (1g sugars, 1g fiber), 3g pro.

READER REVIEW
"This recipe is so simple! Delicious for Saturday morning breakfast—with an extra loaf to share with the neighbor!"
—CHERRYLADY, TASTEOFHOME.COM

Sunflower Seed & Honey Wheat Bread

I've tried other bread recipes, but this one is a staple in our home.
I won $50 in a baking contest with a loaf that I had stored in the freezer!
—*Mickey Turner, Grants Pass, OR*

PREP: 40 MIN. + RISING • **BAKE:** 35 MIN. • **MAKES:** 3 LOAVES (12 SLICES EACH)

2 pkg. (¼ oz. each) active dry yeast
3¼ cups warm water (110° to 115°)
¼ cup bread flour
⅓ cup canola oil
⅓ cup honey
3 tsp. salt
6½ to 7½ cups whole wheat flour
½ cup sunflower kernels
3 Tbsp. butter, melted

1. In a large bowl, dissolve yeast in warm water. Add the bread flour, oil, honey, salt and 4 cups of the whole wheat flour. Beat until smooth. Stir in sunflower kernels and enough of the remaining flour to form a firm dough.

2. Turn dough onto a floured surface; knead until smooth and elastic, 6-8 minutes. Place in a greased bowl, turning once to grease the top. Cover and let rise in a warm place until doubled, about 1 hour.

3. Punch dough down; divide into 3 portions. Shape into loaves; place in 3 greased 8x4-in. loaf pans. Cover and let rise until doubled, about 30 minutes.

4. Bake at 350° until golden brown, 35-40 minutes. Brush with melted butter. Remove from pans to wire racks to cool.

FREEZE OPTION: Securely wrap and freeze cooled loaves in foil, and place in resealable plastic freezer bags. To use, thaw at room temperature.

1 SLICE: 125 cal., 4g fat (1g sat. fat), 3mg chol., 212mg sod., 19g carb. (3g sugars, 3g fiber), 4g pro. **DIABETIC EXCHANGES:** 1 starch, 1 fat.

Dill Batter Bread

Even those who don't consider themselves bakers can make
this bread with success. And your guests will be delighted!
—*Donna Lindecamp, Morganton, NC*

PREP: 15 MIN. + RISING • **BAKE:** 45 MIN. + COOLING • **MAKES:** 16 SERVINGS

¼ cup sugar
2 pkg. (¼ oz. each) active
 dry yeast
2 tsp. dill weed
1½ tsp. salt
4½ cups all-purpose flour
1 cup water
1 cup 2% milk
¼ cup canola oil
1 large egg, room
 temperature
2 tsp. butter, melted
½ tsp. kosher salt

1. In a large bowl, mix the sugar, yeast, dill weed, salt and 2 cups flour. In a small saucepan, heat water, milk and oil to 120°-130°. Add to the dry ingredients; beat on medium speed 2 minutes. Add the egg; beat on high 2 minutes. Stir in the remaining flour to form a stiff batter. Cover and let rise until doubled, about 1 hour.

2. Preheat oven to 375°. Stir down batter. Transfer to a greased 2½-qt. round baking dish. Bake 45-50 minutes or until deep golden brown and bread sounds hollow when tapped.

3. Cool 5 minutes before removing to a wire rack. Brush with butter; sprinkle with salt. Cool completely.

1 PIECE: 191 cal., 5g fat (1g sat. fat), 14mg chol., 298mg sod., 31g carb. (4g sugars, 1g fiber), 5g pro.

NOTES

Crusty Homemade Cheddar Cheese Bread

Crackling homemade bread makes an average day extraordinary. You can leave out the cheese to make a classic loaf, or stir in a few favorites like garlic, herbs and dried fruits.
—*Megumi Garcia, Milwaukee, WI*

PREP: 20 MIN. + CHILLING • **BAKE:** 50 MIN. • **MAKES:** 1 LOAF (16 SLICES)

1½ tsp. active dry yeast
1¾ cups water (70° to 75°)
3½ cups plus 1 Tbsp. all-purpose flour, divided
2 tsp. salt
1 Tbsp. cornmeal or additional
4 oz. sharp cheddar cheese, diced flour

FOR CLASSIC CRUSTY BREAD:

Prepare the dough as directed. After refrigerating dough overnight, knead and shape as directed, omitting the cheese.

FOR RUSTIC CRANBERRY & ORANGE BREAD:

Prepare the dough as directed. After refrigerating dough overnight, knead in 1 cup dried cranberries and 4 tsp. grated orange zest before shaping.

1. In a small bowl, dissolve yeast in water. In a large bowl, mix 3½ cups of flour and the salt. Using a rubber spatula, stir in the yeast mixture to form a soft, sticky dough. Do not knead. Cover and let rise at room temperature 1 hour.

2. Punch down dough. Turn onto a lightly floured surface; pat into a 9-in. square. Fold square into thirds, forming a 9x3-in. rectangle. Fold rectangle into thirds, forming a 3-in. square. Turn dough over; place in a greased bowl, turning once to grease the top. Cover and let rise at room temperature until almost doubled, about 1 hour.

3. Punch down dough and repeat the folding process. Return dough to the bowl; refrigerate, covered, overnight.

4. Dust bottom of a disposable foil roasting pan with cornmeal. Turn dough onto a floured surface. Knead gently 6-8 times, add diced cheese and shape into a 6-in. round loaf. Place in prepared pan; dust top with the remaining 1 Tbsp. flour. Cover pan and let rise at room temperature until dough expands to a 7½-in. loaf, about 1¼ hours.

5. Preheat oven to 500°. Using a sharp knife, make a shallow slash (¼ in. deep) across top of loaf. Cover pan tightly with foil. Bake on lowest oven rack 25 minutes.

6. Reduce oven setting to 450°. Remove foil; bake bread until deep golden brown, 25-30 minutes. Remove to a wire rack to cool.

1 SLICE: 105 cal., 0 fat (0 sat. fat), 0 chol., 296mg sod., 22g carb. (0 sugars, 1g fiber), 3g pro.

Cheese Batter Bread

This bread has a distinctive flavor and will become a family favorite.
Slices pair well with chili in place of the usual cornbread.
—*Shirley Ramsey, Wymore, NE*

PREP: 20 MIN. + RISING • **BAKE:** 25 MIN. • **MAKES:** 1 LOAF (16 SLICES)

1 pkg. (¼ oz.) active
  dry yeast
1 cup warm chicken
  broth (110° to 115°)
2 Tbsp. sugar
1 Tbsp. butter
½ tsp. salt
½ tsp. poultry seasoning
1 large egg, room
  temperature, beaten
3 cups all-purpose flour,
  divided
1¼ cups finely shredded
  cheddar cheese,
  divided
  Onion salt, optional

1. In a large bowl, dissolve yeast in warm broth. Add the sugar, butter, salt, poultry seasoning, egg and 1 cup of flour; beat until smooth. Add 1 cup of cheese and the remaining flour; stir for 1 minute.

2. Cover and let rise in a warm place until doubled, about 30 minutes. Stir the batter down, about 25 strokes. Spread evenly into a greased 9x5-in. loaf pan. Cover and let rise until doubled, about 20 minutes.

3. Sprinkle with the remaining cheese; sprinkle with onion salt if desired. Bake at 375° for 25-30 minutes or until golden brown. Remove from pan to a wire rack. Serve warm. Refrigerate leftovers.

1 SLICE: 136 cal., 4g fat (2g sat. fat), 25mg chol., 197mg sod., 20g carb. (2g sugars, 1g fiber), 5g pro.

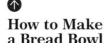

How to Make a Bread Bowl

- Cut a thin slice off the top of bread loaf.

- Hollow out bottom of loaf, leaving a ¼-in.-thick shell. Add soup, stew or chili when ready to serve.

STEAM STRATEGY

To approximate that crackling crust you find on fancy artisanal breads, get steamy. A quick spritz of water into the oven or a light mist sprayed directly on the loaf right before baking should do the trick. Scoring the exterior of the bread creates weak points that help prevent it from bursting and directs expansion to shape the loaf. And it looks really pretty to boot!

Quick & Easy Bread Bowls

Impress your friends by serving cream soups or dips in homemade bread bowls.
I run a food blog, yammiesnoshery.com, and this is one of my most popular recipes.
—*Rachel Preus, Marshall, MI*

PREP: 35 MIN. + RISING • **BAKE:** 20 MIN. + COOLING • **MAKES:** 6 SERVINGS

2 **Tbsp. active dry yeast**
3 **cups warm water
    (110° to 115°)**
2 **Tbsp. sugar**
2 **tsp. salt**
6½ **to 7½ cups bread flour**
   **Optional: Cornmeal and
    sesame seeds**

1. In a small bowl, dissolve yeast in warm water. In a large bowl, combine sugar, salt, yeast mixture and 3 cups flour; beat on medium speed 3 minutes. Stir in enough of the remaining flour to form a soft dough (dough will be sticky).

2. Turn dough onto a floured surface; knead until smooth and elastic, 6-8 minutes. Place in a greased bowl, turning once to grease the top. Cover with a kitchen towel and let rise in a warm place until doubled, about 30 minutes.

3. Preheat oven to 500°. Punch dough down. Divide and shape into 6 balls. Place 3 in. apart on 2 baking sheets that have been generously sprinkled with cornmeal or greased. Cover with a kitchen towel; let rise in a warm place until doubled, about 15 minutes.

4. Spray loaves with water; if desired, generously sprinkle with sesame seeds. Using a sharp knife, score surface with shallow cuts in an "X" pattern. Bake for 2 minutes. Reduce oven setting to 425°. Bake until golden brown and internal temperature reaches 190°-200°. Remove from pans to wire racks to cool.

5. Cut a thin slice off the top of bread. Hollow out bottom portion of loaf, leaving a ¼-in. shell. Discard removed bread or save for another use, such as croutons.

1 BREAD BOWL: 283 cal., 1g fat (0 sat. fat), 0 chol., 396mg sod., 57g carb. (2g sugars, 2g fiber), 10g pro.

Vegetable & Cheese Focaccia

My family eats up this flavorful bread as fast as I can make it. Sometimes I add different herbs, red onion or crumbled bacon. It's one of my best recipes!
—*Mary Cass, Baltimore, MD*

PREP: 20 MIN. + RISING • BAKE: 30 MIN. • MAKES: 15 SERVINGS

1 cup water (70° to 80°)
4½ tsp. olive oil
4½ tsp. sugar
2 tsp. dried oregano
1¼ tsp. salt
3¼ cups bread flour
1½ tsp. active dry yeast

TOPPING
1 Tbsp. olive oil
1 Tbsp. dried basil
2 medium tomatoes, thinly sliced
1 medium onion, thinly sliced
1 cup frozen chopped broccoli, thawed
¼ tsp. salt
¼ tsp. pepper
¾ cup grated Parmesan cheese
1 cup shredded part-skim mozzarella cheese

1. In bread machine pan, place the first 7 ingredients in order suggested by manufacturer. Select dough setting (check dough after 5 minutes of mixing; add 1-2 Tbsp. water or flour if needed).

2. When cycle is completed, turn dough onto a lightly floured surface. Punch dough down. Roll into a 13x9-in. rectangle; transfer to a 13x9-in. baking dish coated with cooking spray.

3. For topping, brush dough with olive oil; sprinkle with basil. Layer with the tomatoes, onion and broccoli; sprinkle with salt, pepper and Parmesan cheese. Cover and let rise in a warm place until doubled, about 30 minutes.

4. Bake at 350° for 20 minutes. Sprinkle with mozzarella cheese; bake 10-15 minutes longer or until golden brown and cheese is melted.

1 PIECE: 151 cal., 4g fat (2g sat. fat), 7mg chol., 315mg sod., 22g carb. (3g sugars, 2g fiber), 7g pro.

Seeded Butternut Squash Braid

Green-hulled pumpkin seeds (better known as pepitas) add a slightly nutty taste to this rich bread. Because of their high oil content, pepitas can spoil quickly, so make sure you store them in the freezer to keep them fresh.
—*Cheryl Perry, Hertford, NC*

PREP: 45 MIN. + RISING • **BAKE:** 20 MIN. • **MAKES:** 1 LOAF (18 SLICES)

2¾ cups uncooked cubed peeled butternut squash
1 pkg. (¼ oz.) active dry yeast
⅓ cup warm 2% milk (110° to 115°)
2 Tbsp. warm water (110° to 115°)
½ cup pepitas or sunflower kernels
¼ cup butter, softened
1 large egg, room temperature
3 Tbsp. brown sugar
½ tsp. salt
3½ to 4 cups all-purpose flour

TOPPING
1 large egg
1 Tbsp. water
¼ cup pepitas or sunflower kernels

1. Place squash in a large saucepan and cover with water. Bring to a boil. Reduce heat; cover and cook for 15-20 minutes or until tender. Drain and mash squash (you will need 2 cups); cool to 110°-115°.

2. In a small bowl, dissolve yeast in warm milk and water. In a large bowl, combine the pepitas, butter, egg, brown sugar, salt, cooked squash, yeast mixture and 2 cups flour; beat on medium speed for 3 minutes. Stir in enough of the remaining flour to form a soft dough (dough will be sticky).

3. Turn onto a floured surface; knead until smooth and elastic, 6-8 minutes. Place in a greased bowl, turning once to grease the top. Cover and let rise in a warm place until doubled, about 1 hour.

4. Punch dough down. Turn onto a lightly floured surface; divide into thirds. Shape each portion into a 26-in. rope; braid ropes. Transfer braid to a greased baking sheet; form into a circle, pinching ends together to seal. Cover with a clean kitchen towel; let rise in a warm place until doubled, about 45 minutes.

5. For topping, beat egg and water; brush over braid. Sprinkle with pepitas. Bake at 350° for 18-23 minutes or until golden brown. Remove from pan to wire rack.

1 SLICE: 192 cal., 7g fat (3g sat. fat), 31mg chol., 150mg sod., 25g carb. (4g sugars, 2g fiber), 7g pro. **DIABETIC EXCHANGES:** 1½ starch, 1 fat.

Sourdough French Bread

These tangy, delicious loaves rival any bread found in
stores and can be made with relative ease.
—*Delila George, Junction City, OR*

PREP: 15 MIN. + RISING • **BAKE:** 20 MIN. • **MAKES:** 2 LOAVES (10 SLICES EACH)

1 pkg. (¼ oz.) active
　dry yeast
1¾ cups warm water
　(110° to 115°)
¼ cup SOURDOUGH
　STARTER (p. 26)
2 Tbsp. canola oil
2 Tbsp. sugar
2 tsp. salt
4¼ cups all-purpose flour

CORNSTARCH WASH
½ cup water
1½ tsp. cornstarch

1. In a large mixing bowl, dissolve yeast in warm water. Add the Sourdough Starter, oil, sugar, salt and 3 cups flour. Beat until smooth. Stir in enough additional flour to form a soft dough.

2. Turn onto a floured surface; knead gently 20-30 times (dough will be slightly sticky). Place in a greased bowl, turning once to grease top. Cover and let rise in a warm place until doubled, 1-1½ hours.

3. Preheat oven to 400°. Punch dough down. Turn onto a lightly floured surface; divide in half. Roll each portion into a 12x8-in. rectangle. Roll up each rectangle, jelly-roll style, starting with a long side; pinch ends to seal. Place each roll seam side down on a greased baking sheet; tuck ends under. Cover and let rise until doubled, about 30 minutes.

4. With a sharp knife, make 4 shallow diagonal slashes across the top of each loaf. In a small saucepan, combine water and cornstarch. Cook and stir over medium heat until thickened. Brush some of the cornstarch wash over the loaves.

5. Bake for 15 minutes. Brush loaves with the remaining cornstarch wash. Bake until lightly browned, 5-10 minutes. Remove from pans to wire racks to cool.

1 SLICE: 116 cal., 2g fat (0 sat. fat), 0 chol., 237mg sod., 22g carb. (1g sugars, 1g fiber), 3g pro.

Honey-Squash Dinner Rolls

These puffy dinner rolls take on rich color when you add squash to the dough.
Any squash variety works—I've even used cooked carrots.
—Marcia Whitney, Gainesville, FL

PREP: 40 MIN. + RISING • **BAKE:** 20 MIN. • **MAKES:** 2 DOZEN

- 2 pkg. (¼ oz. each) active dry yeast
- 2 tsp. salt
- ¼ tsp. ground nutmeg
- 6 to 6½ cups all-purpose flour
- 1¼ cups 2% milk
- ½ cup butter, cubed
- ½ cup honey
- 1 pkg. (12 oz.) frozen mashed winter squash, thawed (about 1⅓ cups)
- 1 large egg, lightly beaten
  Poppy seeds, salted pumpkin seeds or pepitas, or sesame seeds

1. In a large bowl, mix yeast, salt, nutmeg and 3 cups flour. In a small saucepan, heat the milk, butter and honey to 120°-130°. Add to dry ingredients; beat on medium speed for 2 minutes. Add squash; beat on high 2 minutes. Stir in enough of the remaining flour to form a soft dough (dough will be sticky).

2. Turn dough onto a floured surface; knead until smooth and elastic, 6-8 minutes. Place in a greased bowl, turning once to grease the top. Cover and let rise in a warm place until doubled, about 1 hour.

3. Punch down dough. Turn onto a lightly floured surface; divide and shape into 24 balls. Divide between 2 greased 9-in. cast-iron skillets or round baking pans. Cover with kitchen towels; let rise in a warm place until doubled, about 45 minutes.

4. Preheat oven to 375°. Brush tops of rolls with beaten egg; sprinkle with seeds. Bake until dark golden brown, 20-25 minutes. Cover loosely with foil during the last 5-7 minutes if needed to prevent overbrowning. Remove from pans to wire racks; serve warm.

1 ROLL: 186 cal., 5g fat (3g sat. fat), 19mg chol., 238mg sod., 32g carb. (6g sugars, 1g fiber), 4g pro. **DIABETIC EXCHANGES:** 2 starch, 1 fat.

Cheese & Garlic Biscuits

My biscuits won their division at my county fair. One of the judges liked them so much, she asked for the recipe! These buttery, savory biscuits go with just about anything.
—*Gloria Jarrett, Loveland, OH*

TAKES: 20 MIN. • MAKES: 2½ DOZEN

2½ cups biscuit/baking mix
¾ cup shredded sharp cheddar cheese
1 tsp. garlic powder
1 tsp. ranch salad dressing mix
1 cup buttermilk

TOPPING
½ cup butter, melted
1 Tbsp. minced chives
½ tsp. garlic powder
½ tsp. ranch salad dressing mix
¼ tsp. pepper

1. Preheat oven to 450°. In a large bowl, combine the baking mix, cheese, garlic powder and salad dressing mix. Stir in buttermilk just until moistened. Drop by tablespoonfuls onto greased baking sheets.

2. Bake until golden brown, 6-8 minutes. Meanwhile, combine the topping ingredients. Brush over biscuits. Serve warm.

1 BISCUIT: 81 cal., 5g fat (3g sat. fat), 11mg chol., 176mg sod., 7g carb. (1g sugars, 0 fiber), 2g pro.

NOTES

Easy Batter Rolls

The first thing my guests ask when they come for dinner is if I'm serving these dinner rolls. They are so light, airy and delicious that I'm constantly sharing the recipe.
—*Thomasina Brunner, Gloversville, NY*

PREP: 30 MIN. + RISING • **BAKE:** 15 MIN. • **MAKES:** 1 DOZEN

3 cups all-purpose flour
2 Tbsp. sugar
1 pkg. (¼ oz.) active dry yeast
1 tsp. salt
1 cup water
2 Tbsp. butter
1 large egg, room temperature
   Melted butter

1. In a large bowl, combine 2 cups flour, the sugar, yeast and salt. In a saucepan, heat the water and butter to 120°-130°. Add to dry ingredients; beat until blended. Add egg; beat on low speed for 30 seconds, then on high for 3 minutes. Stir in the remaining flour (batter will be stiff). Do not knead. Cover and let rise in a warm place until doubled, about 30 minutes.

2. Stir dough down. Fill 12 greased muffin cups half full. Cover and let rise until doubled, about 15 minutes.

3. Bake at 350° until golden brown, 15-20 minutes. Cool for 1 minute before removing from pan to a wire rack. Brush tops with melted butter.

FREEZE OPTION: Freeze cooled rolls in airtight containers. To use, microwave each roll on high for 30-45 seconds or until warmed.

1 ROLL: 147 cal., 3g fat (1g sat. fat), 21mg chol., 219mg sod., 26g carb. (2g sugars, 1g fiber), 4g pro.

Soft Giant Pretzels

My husband, friends and family love these soft, chewy pretzels. Let your machine mix the dough; then all you have to do is shape and bake these fun snacks.
—*Sherry Peterson, Fort Collins, CO*

PREP: 20 MIN. + RISING • BAKE: 10 MIN. • MAKES: 8 PRETZELS

1   cup plus 2 Tbsp. water
    (70° to 80°)
3   cups all-purpose flour
3   Tbsp. brown sugar
1½ tsp. active dry yeast
2   qt. water
½   cup baking soda
    Coarse salt

1. In a bread machine pan, place the first 4 ingredients in order suggested by manufacturer. Select dough setting. Check dough after 5 minutes of mixing; add 1 to 2 Tbsp. water or flour if needed.

2. When cycle is completed, turn dough onto a lightly floured surface. Divide dough into 8 balls. Roll each ball into a 20-in. rope; form into pretzel shape.

3. Preheat oven to 425°. In a large saucepan, bring water and baking soda to a boil. Drop pretzels into boiling water, 2 at a time; boil for 10-15 seconds. Remove with a slotted spoon; drain on paper towels.

4. Place pretzels on greased baking sheets. Bake until golden brown, 8-10 minutes. Spritz or lightly brush with water. Sprinkle with salt.

1 PRETZEL: 193 cal., 1g fat (0 sat. fat), 0 chol., 380mg sod., 41g carb. (5g sugars, 1g fiber), 5g pro.

Apple & Cheddar Mini Scones

Cheese and sage go well with apples, so why not put them all in scones?
These miniature scones make a fall brunch, tailgate or party even more fun.
—Sue Gronholz, Beaver Dam, WI

PREP: 25 MIN. • **BAKE:** 10 MIN. • **MAKES:** 32 SCONES

3 cups all-purpose flour
3 tsp. baking powder
½ tsp. salt
½ tsp. baking soda
1 cup cold butter, cubed
1 large egg, room temperature
¾ cup vanilla yogurt
3 Tbsp. 2% milk, divided
⅓ cup shredded peeled apple
⅓ cup shredded sharp cheddar cheese
1 Tbsp. minced fresh sage
1 Tbsp. sugar

1. Preheat oven to 425°. In a large bowl, whisk flour, baking powder, salt and baking soda. Cut in butter until mixture resembles coarse crumbs. In another bowl, whisk egg, yogurt and 2 Tbsp. milk; stir into the crumb mixture just until moistened. Stir in apple, cheese and sage.

2. Turn dough onto a lightly floured surface; knead gently 10 times. Divide the dough in half; pat each portion into a 6-in. circle. Cut each circle into 8 wedges; cut each wedge in half.

3. Transfer to parchment-lined baking sheets. Brush tops of scones with remaining milk; sprinkle with sugar. Bake 10-12 minutes or until golden brown. Serve warm.

1 MINI SCONE: 109 cal., 7g fat (4g sat. fat), 23mg chol., 159mg sod., 10g carb. (2g sugars, 0 fiber), 2g pro.

FOR REGULAR-SIZE SCONES: Do not cut wedges in half. Bake as directed, increasing baking time to 12-14 minutes. **MAKES:** 16 regular scones.

Skillet Herb Bread

We had a lot of family get-togethers when I was growing up. My grandmother, aunts and mom were all good cooks, and each had her own specialty when it came to bread. But Mom's was my favorite—the flavors call to mind the taste of cornbread stuffing!
—*Shirley Smith, Yorba Linda, CA*

PREP: 10 MIN. • BAKE: 35 MIN. • MAKES: 10 SERVINGS

1½ cups all-purpose flour
2 Tbsp. sugar
4 tsp. baking powder
1½ tsp. salt
1 tsp. rubbed sage
1 tsp. dried thyme
1½ cups yellow cornmeal
1½ cups chopped celery
1 cup chopped onion
1 jar (2 oz.) chopped pimientos, drained
3 large eggs, room temperature, beaten
1½ cups fat-free milk
⅓ cup vegetable oil

Preheat oven to 400°. In a large bowl, combine the flour, sugar, baking powder, salt, sage and thyme. Combine the cornmeal, celery, onion and pimientos; add to dry ingredients and mix well. Add eggs, milk and oil; stir just until moistened. Pour into a greased 10- or 11-in. ovenproof skillet. Bake 35-45 minutes or until bread tests done. Serve warm.

1 SLICE: 275 cal., 9g fat (2g sat. fat), 57mg chol., 598mg sod., 40g carb. (6g sugars, 2g fiber), 7g pro.

READER REVIEW
"You are right—this bread does taste like stuffing! I already have requests to make it again."
—ISOLDA, TASTEOFHOME.COM

Sour Cream Fan Rolls

I received this recipe from a pen pal in Canada. The dough is so easy
to work with, and it makes the lightest yeast rolls. I haven't used
another white bread recipe since I started making this one.
—Carrie Ormsby, West Jordan, UT

PREP: 30 MIN. + RISING • **BAKE:** 20 MIN./BATCH • **MAKES:** ABOUT 2½ DOZEN

7 to 8 cups all-purpose
   flour
½ cup sugar
2 Tbsp. active dry yeast
1½ tsp. salt
¼ tsp. baking powder
2 cups sour cream
1 cup water
6 Tbsp. butter, cubed
2 large eggs, room
   temperature, lightly
   beaten

1. In a large bowl, combine 3½ cups flour, the sugar, yeast, salt and baking powder. In a small saucepan, heat the sour cream, water and butter to 120°-130°; add to the dry ingredients. Beat on medium speed for 2 minutes. Add eggs and ½ cup flour; beat 2 minutes longer. Stir in enough of the remaining flour to form a soft dough.

2. Turn dough onto a floured surface; knead until smooth and elastic, 6-8 minutes. Place in a greased bowl, turning once to grease top. Cover and let rise in a warm place until doubled, about 1 hour.

3. Punch dough down. Turn onto a lightly floured surface; divide in half. Roll each portion into a 23x9-in. rectangle. Cut into 1½-in. strips. Stack 5 strips together; cut into 1½-in. pieces and place cut side up in a greased muffin cup. Repeat with the remaining strips. Cover and let rise until doubled, about 20 minutes.

4. Bake at 350° for 20-25 minutes or until golden brown. Remove from pans to wire racks.

1 ROLL: 182 cal., 6g fat (3g sat. fat), 31mg chol., 158mg sod., 27g carb. (5g sugars, 1g fiber), 4g pro.

Sweet Potato Crescents

These light-as-air crescent rolls make a delightful accompaniment to any menu. I often serve them as part of our Thanksgiving dinner.
—*Rebecca Bailey, Fairbury, NE*

PREP: 30 MIN. + RISING • **BAKE:** 15 MIN. • **MAKES:** 3 DOZEN

2 pkg. (¼ oz. each) active dry yeast
1 cup warm water (110° to 115°)
1 can (15¾ oz.) cut sweet potatoes, drained and mashed
½ cup sugar
½ cup shortening
1 large egg, room temperature
1½ tsp. salt
5 to 5½ cups all-purpose flour
¼ cup butter, melted

1. In a large bowl, dissolve yeast in water; let stand for 5 minutes. Beat in the sweet potatoes, sugar, shortening, egg, salt and 3 cups flour. Add enough of the remaining flour to form a stiff dough.

2. Turn dough onto a floured surface; knead until smooth and elastic, 6-8 minutes. Place in a greased bowl, turning once to grease top. Cover and let rise in a warm place until doubled, about 1 hour.

3. Punch dough down; divide into thirds. Roll each portion into a 12-in. circle; cut each into 12 wedges. Brush with butter. Roll up from the wide end and place, pointed end down, 2 in. apart on greased baking sheets. Cover and let rise until doubled, about 40 minutes.

4. Bake at 375° for 13-15 minutes or until golden brown. Remove from pans to wire racks.

1 ROLL: 123 cal., 4g fat (2g sat. fat), 9mg chol., 119mg sod., 19g carb. (5g sugars, 1g fiber), 2g pro.

DO THE MASH
If you'd like, you can cook and mash fresh sweet potatoes instead of using canned. A standard can of sweet potatoes produces roughly a cup of mashed.

Flaky Whole Wheat Biscuits

Whole wheat flour gives these biscuits a nutty flavor. Ever since I started making these, white flour biscuits just don't taste as good! Pair them with soup or slather them with whipped cream and sweetened berries for a dessert treat.
—*Trisha Kruse, Eagle, ID*

TAKES: 25 MIN. • MAKES: 10 BISCUITS

1 cup all-purpose flour
1 cup whole wheat flour
3 tsp. baking powder
1 Tbsp. brown sugar
1 tsp. baking soda
½ tsp. salt
¼ cup cold butter
1 cup 2% milk

1. Preheat oven to 425°. In a large bowl, combine the first 6 ingredients. Cut in butter until the mixture resembles coarse crumbs. Stir in the milk just until moistened. Turn onto a lightly floured surface; knead 8-10 times.

2. Pat or roll out dough to ½-in. thickness; cut with a floured 2½-in. biscuit cutter. Place 2 in. apart on an ungreased baking sheet.

3. Bake for 8-10 minutes or until golden brown.

1 BISCUIT. 144 cal., 6g fat (3g sat. fat), 14mg chol., 417mg sod., 21g carb. (3g sugars, 2g fiber), 4g pro. **DIABETIC EXCHANGES:** 1½ starch, 1 fat.

Onion Mustard Buns

I'm an avid bread baker and was thrilled to find this recipe. It makes delectably different rolls that are a hit wherever I take them. The onion and mustard flavors go so well with ham or hamburgers and are special enough to serve alongside an elaborate main dish.
—*Melodie Shumaker, Elizabethtown, PA*

PREP: 25 MIN. + RISING • **BAKE:** 20 MIN. • **MAKES:** 2 DOZEN

1 pkg. (¼ oz.) active dry yeast
¼ cup warm water (110° to 115°)
2 cups warm 2% milk (110° to 115°)
3 Tbsp. dried minced onion
3 Tbsp. prepared mustard
2 Tbsp. canola oil
2 Tbsp. sugar
1½ tsp. salt
6 to 6½ cups all-purpose flour
Optional: Beaten egg, poppy seeds and additional dried minced onion

1. In a large bowl, dissolve yeast in water. Add the milk, onion, mustard, oil, sugar, salt and 4 cups flour; beat until smooth. Add enough remaining flour to form a soft dough.

2. Turn dough out onto a floured surface; knead until smooth and elastic, 6-8 minutes. Place in a greased bowl, turning once to grease top. Cover and let rise in a warm place until doubled, about 1 hour.

3. Punch dough down; divide into 24 pieces. Flatten each piece into a 3-in. circle. Place 1 in. apart on greased baking sheets. Cover and let rise until doubled, about 45 minutes. If desired, brush with beaten egg and sprinkle with poppy seeds or dried minced onion.

4. Bake at 350° for 20-25 minutes or until golden brown. Cool on wire racks.

1 BUN: 138 cal., 2g fat (0 sat. fat), 0 chol., 181mg sod., 26g carb. (0 sugars, 0 fiber), 4g pro. **DIABETIC EXCHANGES:** 1½ starch, ½ fat.

Grandma's Onion Squares

My grandma brought this recipe with her when she emigrated from Italy as a young wife and mother. It is still a family favorite.
—*Janet Eddy, Stockton, CA*

PREP: 40 MIN. • **BAKE:** 35 MIN. • **MAKES:** 9 SERVINGS

2 Tbsp. olive oil
2 cups sliced onions
1 tsp. salt, divided
¼ tsp. pepper
2 cups all-purpose flour
3 tsp. baking powder
5 Tbsp. shortening
⅔ cup 2% milk
1 large egg
¾ cup sour cream

1. Preheat oven to 400°. In a large skillet, heat oil over medium heat. Add onions; cook and stir until softened, 8-10 minutes. Reduce heat to medium-low; cook until deep golden brown, 30-40 minutes, stirring occasionally. Stir in ½ tsp. salt and the pepper.

2. Meanwhile, in a large bowl, combine flour, baking powder and the remaining ½ tsp. salt. Cut in shortening until mixture resembles coarse crumbs. Stir in milk just until moistened. Press into a greased 9-in. square baking pan; top with onions.

3. Combine egg and sour cream; spread over the onion layer. Bake until golden brown, 35-40 minutes. Cut into squares. Serve warm.

1 PIECE: 256 cal., 15g fat (5g sat. fat), 27mg chol., 447mg sod., 25g carb. (3g sugars, 1g fiber), 5g pro.

Yogurt Yeast Rolls

Take these fluffy, golden rolls to a potluck and people will snap them up
in a hurry. It's a nice contribution because rolls are easy
to transport and one batch goes a long way.
—*Carol Forcum, Marion, IL*

PREP: 30 MIN. + RISING • **BAKE:** 15 MIN. • **MAKES:** 2 DOZEN

1½ cups whole wheat flour
3¼ cups all-purpose flour,
   divided
2 pkg. (¼ oz. each) active
   dry yeast
2 tsp. salt
½ tsp. baking soda
1½ cups plain yogurt
½ cup water
3 Tbsp. butter
2 Tbsp. honey
   Additional melted
   butter, optional

1. In a large bowl, combine whole wheat flour, ½ cup of the all-purpose flour, the yeast, salt and baking soda. In a saucepan over low heat, heat yogurt, water, butter and honey to 120°-130°. Pour over the dry ingredients; blend well. Beat on medium speed for 3 minutes. Add enough of the remaining all-purpose flour to form a soft dough.

2. Turn dough onto a floured surface; knead until smooth and elastic, 6-8 minutes. Place in a greased bowl, turning once to grease top. Cover and let rise in a warm place until doubled, about 1 hour.

3. Punch dough down. Turn onto a lightly floured surface; divide into 24 portions. Roll each portion into a 10-in. rope. Shape each rope into an S, then coil each end until it touches the center. Place 3 in. apart on greased baking sheets. Cover and let rise until doubled, about 30 minutes.

4. Bake at 400° until golden brown, about 15 minutes. If desired, brush tops with additional butter while warm. Remove from pans to wire racks to cool.

1 ROLL: 115 cal., 2g fat (1g sat. fat), 6mg chol., 245mg sod., 21g carb. (3g sugars, 1g fiber), 3g pro. **DIABETIC EXCHANGES:** 1½ starch, ½ fat.

Hurry-Up Biscuits

When I was young, my mom would make these biscuits with fresh cream she got from a local farmer. I don't go to those lengths anymore, but this family recipe is still a real treat.
—*Beverly Sprague, Baltimore, MD*

TAKES: 30 MIN. • **MAKES:** 1 DOZEN

3 cups all-purpose flour
4 tsp. baking powder
4 tsp. sugar
1 tsp. salt
2 cups heavy whipping cream

1. Preheat oven to 375°. In a large bowl, whisk the flour, baking powder, sugar and salt. Add cream; stir just until moistened.

2. Drop dough by ¼ cupfuls 1 in. apart onto greased baking sheets. Bake 17-20 minutes or until bottoms are golden brown. Serve warm.

1 BISCUIT: 256 cal., 15g fat (9g sat. fat), 54mg chol., 346mg sod., 26g carb. (2g sugars, 1g fiber), 4g pro.

NOTES

Moist Pumpkin Scones

After trying a pumpkin scone at a coffeehouse, I was inspired to look for
a recipe to try at home. The glaze nicely complements the
pumpkin flavor in these tasty, indulgent treats.
—*Amy McCavour, Gresham, OR*

PREP: 15 MIN. • **BAKE:** 15 MIN. + COOLING • **MAKES:** 16 SCONES

4½ cups all-purpose flour
½ cup packed brown
    sugar
4 tsp. baking powder
3 tsp. pumpkin pie spice
1 tsp. ground cinnamon
½ tsp. baking soda
½ tsp. salt
1 cup cold butter
2 large eggs, room
    temperature
1¼ cups canned pumpkin
¾ cup 2% milk, divided

GLAZE
2 cups confectioners'
    sugar
3 Tbsp. 2% milk
¼ tsp. pumpkin pie spice

1. Preheat oven to 400°. In a large bowl, combine the first 7 ingredients. Cut in butter until mixture resembles coarse crumbs. In another bowl, whisk the eggs, pumpkin and ½ cup milk. Stir into dry ingredients just until moistened.

2. Turn dough onto a floured surface; knead 10 times. Divide dough in half. Pat each portion into an 8-in. circle; cut each into 8 wedges. Separate wedges and place 1 in. apart on ungreased baking sheets. Brush with the remaining milk.

3. Bake for 12-15 minutes or until golden brown. Remove to wire racks; cool for 10 minutes. Combine the glaze ingredients; drizzle over scones. Serve warm.

1 SCONE: 338 cal., 13g fat (8g sat. fat), 59mg chol., 348mg sod., 51g carb. (23g sugars, 2g fiber), 5g pro.

Jumbo Jalapeno Cheddar Rolls

Add some excitement to your Christmas or New Year's spread
with these colorful rolls. The cheddar and jalapeno flavors
are mild, but everyone loves the zesty taste.
—*Linda Foreman, Locust Grove, OK*

PREP: 35 MIN. + RISING • **BAKE:** 20 MIN. • **MAKES:** 1 DOZEN

2 **pkg. (¼ oz. each) active dry yeast**
2 **Tbsp. sugar**
2 **cups warm whole milk (110° to 115°)**
2 **large eggs, room temperature**
2 **tsp. salt**
6½ **to 7½ cups all-purpose flour**
2 **cups shredded cheddar cheese**
¼ **cup chopped seeded jalapeno pepper**

EGG WASH
1 **large egg**
2 **tsp. water**

1. In a large bowl, dissolve yeast and sugar in warm milk. Add the eggs, salt and 4 cups flour. Beat on medium speed for 3 minutes. Add cheese and jalapeno. Stir in enough of the remaining flour to form a firm dough.

2. Turn dough onto a floured surface; knead until smooth and elastic, 6-8 minutes. Place in a greased bowl, turning once to grease the top. Cover and let rise in a warm place until doubled, about 1 hour.

3. Punch dough down. Turn onto a lightly floured surface; divide into 12 pieces. Shape each piece into a roll. Place 3 in. apart on lightly greased baking sheets. Cover and let rise until doubled, about 30 minutes.

4. Combine egg and water; brush over rolls. Bake at 375° for 16-20 minutes or until golden brown. Remove from pans to wire racks. Serve warm.

1 ROLL: 368 cal., 9g fat (5g sat. fat), 77mg chol., 542mg sod., 57g carb. (5g sugars, 2g fiber), 14g pro.

Homemade Tortillas

I usually have to double this recipe because we go through these so quickly!
The tortillas are so tender, chewy and simple, you'll never use store-bought again.
—*Kristin Van Dyken, Kennewick, WA*

TAKES: 30 MIN. • MAKES: 8 TORTILLAS

2   cups all-purpose flour
½   tsp. salt
¾   cup water
3   Tbsp. olive oil

NO PUFF? NO PROBLEM!
Your tortillas should puff up slightly as they cook, forming a few large bubbles. If your tortillas aren't puffing, either they're too thick, or your temperature is too low.

1. In a large bowl, combine flour and salt. Stir in water and oil. Turn onto a floured surface; knead 10-12 times, adding a little flour or water if needed to achieve a smooth dough. Let rest for 10 minutes.

2. Divide dough into 8 portions. On a lightly floured surface, roll each portion into a 7-in. circle.

3. In a greased cast-iron or other heavy skillet, cook the tortillas over medium heat until lightly browned, 1 minute on each side. Serve warm.

1 TORTILLA: 159 cal., 5g fat (1g sat. fat), 0 chol., 148mg sod., 24g carb. (1g sugars, 1g fiber), 3g pro. **DIABETIC EXCHANGES:** 1½ starch, 1 fat.

Onion & Garlic Biscuits

Bake a dozen of these oniony, herby biscuits for a little something new in the holiday bread basket. They're also awesome with a bowl of chili, soup or stew.
—*L. Dorow, Fairmont, MN*

TAKES: 20 MIN. • MAKES: 1 DOZEN

1 **Tbsp. canola oil**
1 **medium onion, finely chopped**
2 **garlic cloves, minced**
2 **cups biscuit/baking mix**
½ **tsp. dried thyme**
⅔ **cup 2% milk**

1. Preheat oven to 450°. In a skillet, heat oil over medium heat. Add onion; cook and stir 3-4 minutes or until tender. Stir in garlic; cook 1 minute longer. Cool completely.

2. In a large bowl, combine baking mix, thyme and onion mixture; make a well in center. Pour milk into well; stir just until moistened. Drop dough by rounded tablespoonfuls 2 in. apart onto a greased baking sheet.

3. Bake 8-10 minutes or until golden brown. Serve warm.

1 BISCUIT: 101 cal., 4g fat (2g sat. fat), 4mg chol., 262mg sod., 15g carb. (2g sugars, 1g fiber), 2g pro.

Grandma's Rosemary Dinner Rolls

My baba made these in her coal oven. How she regulated the temperature is beyond me!
She always made extra rolls for the neighbors to bake in their own ovens.
At lunchtime, my mom and aunts delivered the formed rolls.
—*Charlotte Hendershot, Hudson, PA*

PREP: 35 MIN. + RISING • **BAKE:** 20 MIN. • **MAKES:** 1 DOZEN

- 1 **pkg. (¼ oz.) active dry yeast**
- ¼ **cup warm water (110° to 115°)**
- 3 **cups bread flour**
- 2 **Tbsp. sugar**
- 1 **Tbsp. minced fresh rosemary, divided**
- ¾ **tsp. salt**
- ⅔ **cup warm 2% milk (110° to 115°)**
- 1 **large egg, room temperature**
- ¼ **to ⅓ cup canola oil**

EGG WASH
- 1 **large egg yolk**
- 2 **Tbsp. 2% milk**

1. In a small bowl, dissolve yeast in warm water. Place the flour, sugar, 2 tsp. rosemary and the salt in a food processor; pulse until blended. Add the warm milk, egg and yeast mixture; cover and pulse 10 times or until almost blended.

2. While processing, gradually add oil just until dough pulls away from sides and begins to form a ball. Process 2 minutes longer to knead dough (dough will be very soft).

3. Transfer dough to a greased bowl, turning once to grease the top. Cover and let rise in a warm place until doubled, about 1 hour.

4. Punch down dough. Turn onto a lightly floured surface; divide and shape into 12 balls. Roll each ball into a 15-in. rope. Starting at 1 end, loosely wrap dough around itself to form a coil. Tuck end under; pinch to seal. Repeat to coil the remaining ropes.

5. Place 2 in. apart on greased baking sheets. Cover and let rise until doubled, about 30 minutes.

6. Preheat oven to 350°. In a small bowl, whisk the egg yolk and milk; brush over rolls. Sprinkle with remaining rosemary. Bake until golden brown, 18-22 minutes. Remove from pans to wire racks; serve warm.

1 ROLL: 194 cal., 6g fat (1g sat. fat), 32mg chol., 163mg sod., 28g carb. (3g sugars, 1g fiber), 6g pro.

Wonderful English Muffins

When I was growing up on a farm, my mom always seemed to be making homemade bread...nothing tasted so good! Now I like to make these simple yet delicious muffins for my own family.
—*Linda Rasmussen, Twin Falls, ID*

PREP: 30 MIN. + RISING • **COOK:** 25 MIN. • **MAKES:** 12 MUFFINS

1 cup whole milk
¼ cup butter, cubed
2 Tbsp. sugar
1 tsp. salt
2 pkg. (¼ oz. each) active
   dry yeast
1 cup warm water
   (110° to 115°)
2 cups all-purpose flour
3 to 3½ cups whole
   wheat flour
1 Tbsp. sesame seeds
1 Tbsp. poppy seeds
   Cornmeal

1. Scald milk in a saucepan; add butter, sugar and salt. Stir until butter melts; cool to lukewarm.

2. In a small bowl, dissolve yeast in warm water; add to the milk mixture. Stir in all-purpose flour and 1 cup whole wheat flour until smooth. Add sesame seeds, poppy seeds and enough of the remaining whole wheat flour to make a soft dough.

3. Turn dough onto a floured surface; knead until smooth and elastic, 8-10 minutes. Place in a greased bowl, turning once to grease top. Cover and let rise until doubled, about 1 hour.

4. Punch dough down. Roll to ⅓-in. thickness on a cornmeal-covered surface. Cut into circles with a 3½-in. or 4-in. cutter; cover with a towel and let rise until nearly doubled, about 30 minutes.

5. Place muffins, cornmeal side down, in a greased skillet; cook over medium-low heat for 12-14 minutes or until bottoms are browned. Turn and cook about 12-14 minutes or until browned. Cool the muffins on wire racks; split and toast to serve.

1 MUFFIN: 240 cal., 6g fat (3g sat. fat), 13mg chol., 248mg sod., 41g carb. (4g sugars, 4g fiber), 7g pro.

NOTES

Apple Cider Biscuits

My family enjoys these tender, flaky biscuits warm from the oven.
We have a lot of apple trees, so we're always looking for
apple recipes. This is a tasty way to use some of our cider.
—Harriet Stichter, Milford, IN

TAKES: 30 MIN. • **MAKES:** ABOUT 1 DOZEN

2 cups all-purpose flour
1 Tbsp. baking powder
2 tsp. sugar
½ tsp. salt
⅓ cup cold butter
¾ cup apple cider
⅛ tsp. ground cinnamon
Honey, optional

1. Preheat oven to 425°. In a bowl, combine the flour, baking powder, sugar and salt. Cut in butter until mixture resembles coarse crumbs. Stir in apple cider just until moistened. Turn onto a lightly floured surface and knead 8-10 times.

2. Roll out dough to ½-in. thickness; cut with a 2½-in. biscuit cutter. Place on ungreased baking sheets. Sprinkle with cinnamon; pierce tops of biscuits with a fork.

3. Bake for 12-14 minutes or until golden brown. If desired, serve with honey.

1 BISCUIT: 131 cal., 5g fat (3g sat. fat), 14mg chol., 252mg sod., 18g carb. (3g sugars, 1g fiber), 2g pro.

Stollen Butter Rolls

Our family enjoys my stollen so much that it's just too good to be served only as a holiday sweet bread. I created this buttery, less-sweet dinner roll so we can satisfy our stollen cravings anytime.
—*Mindy White, Nashville, TN*

PREP: 45 MIN. + RISING • **BAKE:** 15 MIN. • **MAKES:** 2 DOZEN

1 pkg. (¼ oz.) active dry yeast
¼ cup warm water (110° to 115°)
1 cup 2% milk
2 large eggs, room temperature
½ cup butter, softened
1 Tbsp. sugar
1 tsp. salt
4¼ to 4¾ cups all-purpose flour
¾ cup chopped mixed candied fruit
¾ cup dried currants
½ cup cold butter, cut into 24 pieces (1 tsp. each)

1. In a small bowl, dissolve yeast in warm water. In a large bowl, combine milk, eggs, butter, sugar, salt, yeast mixture and 3 cups flour; beat on medium speed until smooth. Stir in enough of the remaining flour to form a soft dough (dough will be sticky).

2. Turn out the dough onto a floured surface; knead until smooth and elastic, 6-8 minutes. Place in a greased bowl, turning once to grease the top. Cover and let rise in a warm place until doubled, about 1 hour.

3. Punch dough down, turn out onto a floured surface. Knead candied fruit and currants into the dough (knead in more flour if necessary).

4. Divide and shape into 24 balls; flatten slightly into circles. Place 1 tsp. cold butter in center of each circle. Fold circles in half over butter; press edges to seal. Place in a greased 15x10x1-in. baking pan. Cover and let rise in a warm place until doubled, about 45 minutes.

5. Bake at 375° until golden brown, 15-20 minutes. Cool in pan 5 minutes; serve warm.

FREEZE OPTION: Freeze cooled rolls in airtight containers. To use, microwave each roll on high for 30-45 seconds until warmed.

1 ROLL: 198 cal., 9g fat (5g sat. fat), 37mg chol., 178mg sod., 28g carb. (9g sugars, 1g fiber), 4g pro.

Apple Streusel Muffins

These muffins remind us of coffee cake, and my husband and kids love them as a quick breakfast or snack on the run. The drizzle of glaze makes them pretty enough for company.
—*Dulcy Grace, Roaring Spring, PA*

PREP: 20 MIN. • BAKE: 15 MIN. • MAKES: 1 DOZEN

- 2 cups all-purpose flour
- 1 cup sugar
- 1 tsp. baking powder
- ½ tsp. baking soda
- ½ tsp. salt
- 2 large eggs, room temperature
- ½ cup butter, melted
- 1¼ tsp. vanilla extract
- 1½ cups peeled chopped tart apples

STREUSEL TOPPING
- ⅓ cup packed brown sugar
- 1 Tbsp. all-purpose flour
- ⅛ tsp. ground cinnamon
- 1 Tbsp. cold butter

GLAZE
- ¾ cup confectioners' sugar
- 2 to 3 tsp. 2% milk
- 1 tsp. butter, melted
- ⅛ tsp. vanilla extract
- Dash salt

1. Preheat oven to 375°. Whisk together first 5 ingredients. In another bowl, whisk together eggs, melted butter and vanilla; add to flour mixture, stirring just until moistened (batter will be stiff). Fold in apples. Fill 12 greased or paper-lined muffin cups three-fourths full.

2. For topping, mix brown sugar, flour and cinnamon; cut in butter until crumbly. Sprinkle over batter.

3. Bake until a toothpick inserted in center comes out clean, 15-20 minutes. Cool in pan for 5 minutes before removing to a wire rack to cool. Mix glaze ingredients; drizzle over tops.

1 MUFFIN: 295 cal., 10g fat (6g sat. fat), 55mg chol., 398mg sod., 49g carb. (32g sugars, 1g fiber), 3g pro.

READER REVIEW
"A great recipe for fall! I used gala apples, which are my favorite, and left them in pretty big chunks so you could be sure to get the apple in almost every bite!"
—MRS._WHITE, TASTEOFHOME.COM

Blueberry Quick Bread with Vanilla Sauce

I really love fruit, so I stir 2 cups of blueberries into this bread. The vanilla sauce makes it sweet, almost like dessert. I suggest serving it with a morning coffee.
—*Sue Davis, Wausau, WI*

PREP: 20 MIN. • **BAKE:** 50 MIN. + COOLING • **MAKES:** 8 SERVINGS (2 CUPS SAUCE)

1   **large egg, room temperature**
1   **cup 2% milk**
3   **Tbsp. vegetable oil**
2   **cups all-purpose flour**
1   **cup sugar**
2½ **tsp. baking powder**
½   **tsp. salt**
2   **cups fresh or frozen blueberries**

VANILLA SAUCE
1   **cup sugar**
1   **Tbsp. cornstarch**
1   **cup heavy whipping cream**
½   **cup butter, cubed**
1   **tsp. vanilla extract**

1. Preheat oven to 350°. In a large bowl, beat the egg, milk and oil. Combine the flour, sugar, baking powder and salt; gradually add to the egg mixture, beating just until combined. Fold in blueberries.

2. Pour batter into a greased 9x5-in. loaf pan. Bake for 50-55 minutes or until a toothpick inserted in the center comes out clean. Cool in pan for 10 minutes before removing to a wire rack to cool completely.

3. For sauce, combine sugar and cornstarch in a saucepan. Stir in cream until smooth; add butter. Bring to a boil over medium heat; cook and stir for 2 minutes or until mixture is thickened. Stir in vanilla. Serve with blueberry bread.

FREEZE OPTION: Securely wrap and freeze cooled loaf in foil. To use, thaw at room temperature. Prepare sauce as directed and serve with bread.

1 SLICE: 608 cal., 30g fat (15g sat. fat), 102mg chol., 424mg sod., 82g carb. (55g sugars, 2g fiber), 6g pro.

Cheddar Muffins

A moist, cheesy muffin studded with sweet red pepper and
green onions is so satisfying during the winter months. I recommend
making a double batch because these disappear in a flash!
—*Maria Morelli, Kelowna, BC*

PREP: 20 MIN. • **BAKE:** 15 MIN. • **MAKES:** ABOUT 1 DOZEN

2½ cups all-purpose flour
2 Tbsp. sugar
2 tsp. baking powder
1 tsp. Italian seasoning
½ tsp. baking soda
½ tsp. salt
1 large egg, room
temperature
1½ cups buttermilk
⅓ cup canola oil
2 garlic cloves, minced
2 cups shredded cheddar
cheese
4 green onions, sliced
½ cup finely chopped
sweet red pepper
2 Tbsp. finely chopped
oil-packed sun-dried
tomatoes, patted dry
⅓ cup shredded
Parmesan cheese

1. Preheat oven to 400°. In a large bowl, whisk flour, sugar, baking powder, Italian seasoning, baking soda and salt. In another bowl, whisk egg, buttermilk, oil and garlic until blended. Add to the flour mixture; stir just until moistened. Fold in cheddar cheese, green onions, sweet red pepper and sun-dried tomatoes.

2. Fill greased muffin cups three-fourths full. Sprinkle with Parmesan cheese. Bake 15-18 minutes or until a toothpick inserted in center comes out clean. Cool 5 minutes before removing from pans to wire racks. Serve warm.

1 MUFFIN: 230 cal., 12g fat (4g sat. fat), 32mg chol., 394mg sod., 22g carb. (4g sugars, 1g fiber), 8g pro.

Chocolate Zucchini Bread

I shred and freeze zucchini from my garden each summer so that I can make this bread all winter long. Our family loves this chocolaty treat.
—*Shari McKinney, Birney, MT*

PREP: 15 MIN. • **BAKE:** 50 MIN. + COOLING • **MAKES:** 2 LOAVES (12 SLICES EACH)

2 **cups sugar**
1 **cup canola oil**
3 **large eggs, room temperature**
3 **tsp. vanilla extract**
2½ **cups all-purpose flour**
½ **cup baking cocoa**
1 **tsp. salt**
1 **tsp. baking soda**
1 **tsp. ground cinnamon**
¼ **tsp. baking powder**
2 **cups shredded peeled zucchini**

1. Preheat oven to 350°. In a large bowl, beat the sugar, oil, eggs and vanilla until well blended. Combine the flour, cocoa, salt, baking soda, cinnamon and baking powder; gradually beat into the sugar mixture until blended. Stir in zucchini. Transfer to 2 greased 8x4-in. loaf pans.

2. Bake for 50-55 minutes or until a toothpick inserted in the center comes out clean. Cool for 10 minutes before removing from pans to wire racks to cool completely.

1 SLICE: 209 cal., 10g fat (1g sat. fat), 26mg chol., 165mg sod., 28g carb. (17g sugars, 1g fiber), 3g pro.

READER REVIEW

"I love this bread more than any chocolate cake I've ever eaten. I usually halve the recipe and make one loaf using two eggs. It wouldn't be safe for me to have two loaves of this in the house at one time!"
—BLUESTOCKING, TASTEOFHOME.COM

↑

Make the Perfect Banana Bread

Use a potato masher to quickly mash ripe bananas. Choose bananas that are yellow with lots of brown spots—the kind you'd normally think are too ripe to eat on their own.

This particular recipe calls for walnuts, but you could also fold in shredded coconut or chocolate chips, and then top the bread with those same ingredients, or with coarse sugar, before baking. Yum!

Banana Nut Bread

This quick bread is a family favorite, so I always try to have ripe bananas on hand especially for this recipe. I'm sure your family will love this tasty, nutty bread as much as mine does.
—*Susan Jones, La Grange Park, IL*

PREP: 10 MIN. • BAKE: 50 MIN. + COOLING • MAKES: 1 LOAF (16 SLICES)

¼ cup butter, softened
¾ cup sugar
2 large eggs, room temperature
¾ cup mashed ripe banana (about 1 large)
½ cup sour cream
2¼ cups all-purpose flour
1 tsp. ground cinnamon
¾ tsp. baking soda
½ tsp. salt
½ cup chopped walnuts
Optional: Additional walnuts, semisweet chocolate chips or coarse sugar

1. Preheat oven to 350°. Beat butter and sugar until blended. Add eggs, 1 at a time, beating well after each addition. Stir in banana and sour cream. Whisk together flour, cinnamon, baking soda and salt. Add to butter mixture, stirring just until moistened. Fold in ½ cup chopped walnuts.

2. Transfer to a greased 9x5-in. loaf pan. If desired, sprinkle with additional walnuts.

3. Bake until a toothpick inserted in center comes out clean, 50-60 minutes. Cool in pan 10 minutes before removing to a wire rack to cool.

1 SLICE: 244 cal., 10g fat (4g sat. fat), 52mg chol., 220mg sod., 35g carb. (15g sugars, 1g fiber), 5g pro.

Lemon-Filled Gingerbread Muffins

These seemingly plain gingerbread muffins hide a delicious surprise—
a sweet lemon filling! You can add a frosting or glaze if you prefer, but
the simple appearance makes the surprise all the sweeter.
—Suzette Jury, Keene, CA

PREP: 25 MIN. • BAKE: 15 MIN. • MAKES: 1½ DOZEN

½ **cup butter, softened**
⅔ **cup sugar**
2 **large eggs, room temperature**
½ **cup molasses**
2 **cups all-purpose flour**
1½ **tsp. ground ginger**
1 **tsp. baking soda**
½ **tsp. salt**
½ **tsp. ground allspice**
1 **cup water**

FILLING
4 **oz. cream cheese, softened**
¼ **cup confectioners' sugar**
1 **Tbsp. lemon juice**
2 **tsp. grated lemon zest**

1. Preheat oven to 375°. In a large bowl, cream butter and sugar until light and fluffy, 5-7 minutes. Add eggs, 1 at a time, beating well after each addition. Beat in molasses. In another bowl, whisk flour, ginger, baking soda, salt and allspice; add to the creamed mixture alternately with water, beating after each addition just until combined. (Batter may appear curdled.)

2. Fill paper-lined muffin cups one-fourth full. In a small bowl, beat filling ingredients until blended. Drop filling by rounded teaspoonfuls into the center of each muffin; cover with the remaining batter.

3. Bake until a toothpick inserted in the muffin portion comes out clean, 14-18 minutes. Cool 5 minutes before removing from pans to wire racks. Serve warm.

1 MUFFIN: 188 cal., 8g fat (5g sat. fat), 41mg chol., 207mg sod., 27g carb. (16g sugars, 0 fiber), 3g pro.

Cheesy Garlic Herb Quick Bread

This bread could just be the perfect companion for any dish.
The sharp cheddar cheese makes it irresistible.
—Taste of Home *Test Kitchen*

PREP: 15 MIN. • **BAKE:** 25 MIN. • **MAKES:** 1 LOAF (12 SLICES)

3 cups all-purpose flour
3 Tbsp. sugar
1 Tbsp. baking powder
2 tsp. Italian seasoning
1 tsp. garlic powder
½ tsp. salt
1 large egg, room temperature
1 cup fat-free milk
½ cup canola oil
1 cup shredded sharp cheddar cheese

1. Preheat oven to 350°. In a large bowl, whisk together first 6 ingredients. In another bowl, whisk together egg, milk and oil. Stir in cheese and add to flour mixture; stir just until moistened.

2. Spoon batter into a greased 9-in. cast-iron skillet and bake until a toothpick inserted in center comes out clean, 25-30 minutes.

1 SLICE: 233 cal., 10g fat (2g sat. fat), 25mg chol., 175mg sod., 29g carb. (4g sugars, 1g fiber), 7g pro.

PAN CHANGE-UP
You can bake this in an 8-in. cast-iron skillet instead—just increase the baking time to 45-50 minutes. The recipe also makes great muffins: Spoon the batter into 9 greased muffin cups; bake at 350° until a toothpick inserted in center comes out clean, 25-30 minutes.

Brown Sugar Oat Muffins

With Kansas being one of the top wheat-producing states, it seems only fitting to share a recipe containing whole wheat flour! These are great muffins to have for breakfast or a late-night snack with a cup of hot cocoa.
—Regina Stock, Topeka, KS

TAKES: 35 MIN. • MAKES: 1 DOZEN

1 cup old-fashioned oats
1 cup whole wheat flour
¾ cup packed brown sugar
½ cup all-purpose flour
2 tsp. baking powder
½ tsp. salt
2 large eggs, room temperature
¾ cup 2% milk
¼ cup canola oil
1 tsp. vanilla extract
Optional: Peanut butter and honey

1. Preheat oven to 400°. Mix first 6 ingredients. In another bowl, whisk together eggs, milk, oil and vanilla. Add to the oat mixture; stir just until moistened.

2. Fill greased or paper-lined muffin cups two-thirds full. Bake until a toothpick inserted in center comes out clean, 15-17 minutes.

3. Cool in pans for 5 minutes before removing muffins to a wire rack. Serve warm. If desired, spread with peanut butter and honey.

1 MUFFIN: 192 cal., 7g fat (1g sat. fat), 32mg chol., 202mg sod., 30g carb. (14g sugars, 2g fiber), 4g pro. **DIABETIC EXCHANGES:** 2 starch, 1½ fat.

Chocolate Banana Bran Muffins

So easy to make, these treats are healthy but still satisfy my chocolate-loving family. Stir in raisin bran instead of bran flakes for a little extra flavorful fun.

—*Tracy Chappell, Hamiota, MB*

TAKES: 25 MIN. • **MAKES:** 1 DOZEN

- 1 cup all-purpose flour
- ½ cup sugar
- 2 Tbsp. baking cocoa
- 1 tsp. baking powder
- 1 tsp. baking soda
- ½ tsp. salt
- 1 cup bran flakes
- 2 large eggs, room temperature
- 1 cup mashed ripe bananas (about 2 medium)
- ⅓ cup canola oil
- ¼ cup buttermilk

1. Preheat oven to 400°. In a large bowl, whisk together the first 6 ingredients. Stir in bran flakes. In another bowl, whisk eggs, bananas, oil and buttermilk until blended. Add to the flour mixture; stir just until moistened.

2. Fill foil-lined muffin cups three-fourths full. Bake until a toothpick inserted in the center of a muffin comes out clean, 12-14 minutes. Cool 5 minutes before removing muffins from pan to a wire rack. Serve warm.

1 MUFFIN: 169 cal., 7g fat (1g sat. fat), 35mg chol., 278mg sod., 24g carb. (12g sugars, 2g fiber), 3g pro. **DIABETIC EXCHANGES:** 1½ starch, 1½ fat.

NOTES

Key Lime Bread

I first tasted this deliciously different bread at a friend's house, and she graciously shared the recipe with me. It's so easy to make and absolutely yummy!
—*Joan Hallford, North Richland Hills, TX*

PREP: 15 MIN. • **BAKE:** 50 MIN. + COOLING • **MAKES:** 2 LOAVES (16 SLICES EACH)

⅔ cup butter, softened
2 cups sugar
4 large eggs, room temperature
2 Tbsp. grated lime zest
2 Tbsp. Key lime juice
1 tsp. vanilla extract
3 cups all-purpose flour
3 tsp. baking powder
1 tsp. salt
1 cup 2% milk
1 cup chopped walnuts

GLAZE
⅔ cup confectioners' sugar
1 to 2 Tbsp. Key lime juice

1. Preheat oven to 350°. In a large bowl, cream butter and sugar until light and fluffy, 5-7 minutes. Beat in eggs. Beat in lime zest, juice and vanilla. Combine the flour, baking powder and salt; gradually add to the creamed mixture alternately with milk, beating well after each addition. Fold in walnuts.

2. Transfer batter to 2 greased 9x5-in. loaf pans. Bake 50-55 minutes or until a toothpick inserted in center comes out clean. Cool 10 minutes before removing from pans to wire racks.

3. For the glaze, combine confectioners' sugar and enough lime juice to reach desired consistency; drizzle over warm bread. Cool completely.

FREEZE OPTION: Do not make glaze. Securely wrap cooled loaves in foil, then freeze. To use, thaw at room temperature. Prepare glaze as directed.

1 SLICE: 173 cal., 7g fat (3g sat. fat), 37mg chol., 150mg sod., 25g carb. (16g sugars, 1g fiber), 3g pro.

Ginger Pear Muffins

This wonderful recipe has been in my files for years.
The chunks of fresh pear make each bite moist and delicious.
—*Lorraine Caland, Shuniah, ON*

PREP: 25 MIN. • BAKE: 20 MIN. • MAKES: 1½ DOZEN

¾ cup packed brown
    sugar
⅓ cup canola oil
1 large egg, room
    temperature
1 cup buttermilk
2½ cups all-purpose flour
1 tsp. baking soda
1 tsp. ground ginger
½ tsp. salt
½ tsp. ground cinnamon
2 cups chopped peeled
    fresh pears

TOPPING
⅓ cup packed brown
    sugar
¼ tsp. ground ginger
2 tsp. butter, melted

1. Preheat oven to 350°. In a small bowl, beat brown sugar, oil and egg until well blended. Beat in the buttermilk. In a small bowl, combine flour, baking soda, ginger, salt and cinnamon; gradually beat into the buttermilk mixture until blended. Stir in the pears. Fill 18 paper-lined muffin cups two-thirds full.

2. For topping, combine brown sugar and ginger. Stir in butter until crumbly. Sprinkle over batter.

3. Bake 18-22 minutes or until a toothpick inserted in the center comes out clean. Cool 5 minutes before removing from pans to wire racks. Serve warm

1 MUFFIN: 174 cal., 5g fat (1g sat. fat), 13mg chol., 162mg sod., 30g carb. (16g sugars, 1g fiber), 3g pro. **DIABETIC EXCHANGES:** 2 starch, 1 fat.

Cranberry Orange Walnut Bread

This bread is a given at our house in Oregon, one of the top cranberry-producing states. Each fall my husband and I scrounge around for walnuts for the recipe. It's a regular on our table, and not just at Thanksgiving. I freeze the berries so I have a ready supply all year long.
—*Elaine Kremenak, Grants Pass, OR*

PREP: 20 MIN. • **BAKE:** 1 HOUR + COOLING • **MAKES:** 1 LOAF (16 SERVINGS)

2 cups all-purpose flour
1 cup sugar
1½ tsp. baking powder
1 tsp. baking soda
½ tsp. salt
1 large egg, room temperature
½ cup orange juice
Grated zest of 1 orange
2 Tbsp. butter, melted
2 Tbsp. hot water
1 cup fresh or frozen cranberries
1 cup coarsely chopped walnuts

1. Preheat oven to 325°. In a large bowl, combine the dry ingredients. In a second bowl, beat the egg. Add orange juice, zest, butter and hot water. Add to the flour mixture, stirring just until moistened. Gently fold in the cranberries and walnuts.

2. Spoon batter into a greased 9x5-in. loaf pan. Bake for 1 hour or until a toothpick inserted in the center comes out clean. Cool for 10 minutes before removing from pan to a wire rack.

1 SLICE: 177 cal., 6g fat (1g sat. fat), 17mg chol., 209mg sod., 27g carb. (14g sugars, 1g fiber), 4g pro.

⊙

How to Make the Best Irish Soda Bread

1. Use a whisk to combine the dry ingredients so that they are evenly distributed and full of air.

2. Divide butter into small cubes. Use a pastry blender, the back of a fork or your fingers to work the butter into the dry ingredients.

3. Knead gently until the dough feels soft and gently pliable. Shape it into a round loaf by pushing your hands underneath the dough. Don't overwork the dough.

4. The egg wash on top will give the loaf a shiny, golden brown finish. Feel free to make more cuts in the surface before baking to "pinch the fairies out."

Classic Irish Soda Bread

This traditional Irish soda bread can be made with an assortment of mix-ins such as dried fruit and nuts, but I like it best with a handful of raisins. It's the perfect change-of-pace item to bring to a get-together.
—Gloria Warczak, Cedarburg, WI

PREP: 15 MIN. • **BAKE:** 30 MIN. • **MAKES:** 8 SERVINGS

2 cups all-purpose flour
2 Tbsp. brown sugar
1 tsp. baking powder
1 tsp. baking soda
½ tsp. salt
3 Tbsp. cold butter, cubed
2 large eggs, room temperature, divided use
¾ cup buttermilk
⅓ cup raisins

1. Preheat oven to 375°. Whisk together first 5 ingredients. Cut in butter until mixture resembles coarse crumbs. In another bowl, whisk together 1 egg and buttermilk. Add to the flour mixture; stir just until moistened. Stir in raisins.

2. Turn dough onto a lightly floured surface; knead gently 6-8 times. Shape into a 6½-in. round loaf; place on a greased baking sheet. Using a sharp knife, make a shallow cross in top of loaf. Whisk remaining egg; brush over top.

3. Bake until golden brown, 30-35 minutes. Remove from pan to a wire rack. Serve warm.

1 PIECE: 210 cal., 6g fat (3g sat. fat), 59mg chol., 463mg sod., 33g carb. (8g sugars, 1g fiber), 6g pro.

CARAWAY IRISH SODA BREAD: Add 1 to 2 Tbsp. caraway seeds to the dry ingredients.

Fresh Pear Bread

When our tree branches are loaded with ripe, juicy pears, I treat my family and friends to loaves of this cinnamony bread that's richly studded with walnuts and pears. I always receive raves and requests for the recipe.

—*Linda Patrick, Houston, TX*

PREP: 15 MIN. • **BAKE:** 55 MIN. + COOLING • **MAKES:** 2 LOAVES (16 SLICES EACH)

3   large eggs, room temperature
1½ cups sugar
¾   cup vegetable oil
1   tsp. vanilla extract
3   cups all-purpose flour
2   tsp. baking powder
2   tsp. ground cinnamon
1   tsp. baking soda
1   tsp. salt
4   cups finely chopped peeled ripe pears (about 4 medium)
1   tsp. lemon juice
1   cup chopped walnuts

1. Preheat oven to 350°. In a bowl, combine the eggs, sugar, oil and vanilla; mix well. Combine flour, baking powder, cinnamon, baking soda and salt; stir into the egg mixture just until moistened. Toss pears with lemon juice. Stir pears and walnuts into batter (batter will be thick).

2. Spoon into 2 greased 9x5-in. loaf pans. Bake for 55-60 minutes or until a toothpick inserted in the center comes out clean. Cool for 10 minutes before removing from pans to wire racks.

1 SLICE: 168 cal., 8g fat (1g sat. fat), 20mg chol., 144mg sod., 22g carb. (12g sugars, 1g fiber), 3g pro.

PICKING YOUR PEARS
For nice, firm (but not too firm!) pear chunks, Bosc or Anjou pears are ideal for this bread.

Mini Corn Muffins with Spicy Cheddar Filling

As an Iowa gardener, I like to feature sweet corn in my recipes. These cute, easy-to-eat bites are a fun change from the usual appetizers.
—*Margaret Blair, Lorimor, IA*

PREP: 30 MIN. • BAKE: 25 MIN. • MAKES: 4 DOZEN

1½ cups all-purpose flour
1 cup cornmeal
2 tsp. sugar
¾ tsp. baking powder
½ tsp. salt
1 large egg, room temperature
¾ cup 2% milk
¼ cup canola oil
1 can (14¾ oz.) cream-style corn

FILLING
2 cups shredded cheddar cheese
1 can (4 oz.) chopped green chiles
¼ cup diced pimientos
1 tsp. chili powder
¼ tsp. hot pepper sauce

1. Preheat oven to 400°. In a large bowl, whisk the first 5 ingredients. In another bowl, whisk the egg, milk and oil until blended. Add to the flour mixture; stir just until moistened. Fold in corn.

2. Fill greased mini muffin cups three-fourths full. Bake 15-18 minutes or until a toothpick inserted in center comes out clean. Cool 5 minutes before removing from pans to wire racks. Reduce oven setting to 350°.

3. In a large bowl, combine filling ingredients. Using a small melon baller, scoop out the center of each muffin; spoon a rounded teaspoon of filling into the center. Bake for 10-12 minutes or until cheese is melted.

1 MUFFIN: 67 cal., 3g fat (1g sat. fat), 9mg chol., 100mg sod., 8g carb. (1g sugars, 0 fiber), 2g pro.

Sweet Potato Spice Bread

It's a good thing this recipe makes two mini loaves because they'll go fast!
For a small household, eat one loaf now and freeze the other for later.
—*Ronnie Littles, Virginia Beach, VA*

PREP: 15 MIN. • **BAKE:** 25 MIN. + COOLING • **MAKES:** 2 MINI LOAVES (6 SLICES EACH)

1 cup all-purpose flour
1½ tsp. baking powder
¼ tsp. each ground
cinnamon, nutmeg and
allspice
⅛ tsp. salt
1 large egg, room
temperature
⅓ cup mashed sweet
potato
⅓ cup honey
3 Tbsp. canola oil
2 Tbsp. molasses
⅓ cup chopped walnuts

1. Preheat oven to 325°. In a small bowl, combine flour, baking powder, spices and salt. In another small bowl, whisk the egg, sweet potato, honey, oil and molasses. Stir into dry ingredients just until moistened. Fold in walnuts.

2. Transfer to 2 greased 5¾x3x2-in. loaf pans. Bake for 25-30 minutes or until a toothpick inserted in the center comes out clean. Cool for 10 minutes before removing from pans to wire racks.

1 SLICE: 142 cal., 6g fat (1g sat. fat), 18mg chol., 85mg sod., 20g carb. (10g sugars, 1g fiber), 3g pro. **DIABETIC EXCHANGES:** 1½ starch, 1 fat.

READER REVIEW
"Such a great recipe. They were soft, moist and very flavorful. I will make them again, double the recipe for sure and give them as gifts. Thanks for sharing!"
—YUEHCHING, TASTEOFHOME.COM

A Bit Nutty Boston Brown Bread

Hearty and dense, my homemade Boston brown bread features hazelnuts for a delightfully nutty taste. Thick slices pair well with just about anything, from soups, and stews to roasts and casseroles.
—*Lorraine Caland, Shuniah, ON*

PREP: 30 MIN. • **BAKE:** 45 MIN. + COOLING • **MAKES:** 2 LOAVES (12 SLICES EACH)

3 cups whole wheat flour
1 cup all-purpose flour
2½ tsp. baking soda
1 tsp. salt
2½ cups buttermilk
1 cup molasses
1 cup golden raisins
¾ cup chopped hazelnuts

1. Preheat oven to 350°. In a large bowl, combine the flours, baking soda and salt. In a small bowl, whisk buttermilk and molasses. Stir into the dry ingredients just until moistened. Fold in raisins and nuts. Transfer to 2 greased 8x4-in. loaf pans.

2. Bake for 45-50 minutes or until a toothpick inserted in the center comes out clean. Cool for 10 minutes before removing from pans to wire racks.

1 SLICE: 159 cal., 3g fat (0 sat. fat), 1mg chol., 263mg sod., 31g carb. (13g sugars, 3g fiber), 4g pro.

NOTES

Appalachian Cornbread

On this westernmost ridge of the Appalachians, we get abundant rain and sunshine, which allows our children to grow a super sweet corn crop. With staggered plantings, there is enough to eat from mid-July through August, plus plenty to freeze for the long winter. This cornbread is just one way we use some of the bounty!
—*Anne Wiehler, Farmington, PA*

PREP: 15 MIN. • **BAKE:** 20 MIN. • **MAKES:** 9 SERVINGS

2 Tbsp. chopped onion
4 Tbsp. canola oil, divided
1 cup all-purpose flour
1 cup cornmeal
2 Tbsp. sugar
4 tsp. baking powder
½ tsp. salt
2 large eggs, room temperature
1 cup 2% milk
½ cup fresh or frozen corn, thawed
⅓ cup shredded cheddar cheese
¼ cup salsa
2 Tbsp. minced chives

1. Preheat oven to 425°. In a small saucepan, saute onion in 1 Tbsp. oil until tender; set aside.

2. In a large bowl, combine flour, cornmeal, sugar, baking powder and salt. In another bowl, whisk eggs, milk and the remaining oil. Stir in the corn, cheddar cheese, salsa, chives and the reserved onion. Stir into the dry ingredients just until combined.

3. Transfer batter to a greased 9-in. square baking pan. Bake until a toothpick inserted in the center comes out clean and top is lightly browned, 20-25 minutes. Cut into squares; serve warm.

1 PIECE: 229 cal., 10g fat (3g sat. fat), 55mg chol., 395mg sod., 29g carb. (5g sugars, 2g fiber), 6g pro.

Double Chocolate Banana Muffins

Combining two favorite flavors like rich chocolate and soft banana makes these muffins doubly good.
—*Donna Brockett, Kingfisher, OK*

PREP: 15 MIN. • **BAKE:** 20 MIN. • **MAKES:** ABOUT 1 DOZEN

1½ cups all-purpose flour
1 cup sugar
¼ cup baking cocoa
1 tsp. baking soda
½ tsp. salt
¼ tsp. baking powder
1⅓ cups mashed ripe bananas (about 3 medium)
⅓ cup canola oil
1 large egg, room temperature
1 cup miniature semisweet chocolate chips

1. Preheat oven to 350°. Whisk together first 6 ingredients. In a separate bowl, whisk the bananas, oil and egg until blended. Add to the flour mixture; stir just until moistened. Fold in chocolate chips.

2. Fill greased or paper-lined muffin cups three-fourths full. Bake until a toothpick inserted in center comes out clean, 20-25 minutes. Cool 5 minutes before removing from pan to a wire rack. Serve warm.

1 MUFFIN: 278 cal., 11g fat (3g sat. fat), 16mg chol., 220mg sod., 45g carb. (28g sugars, 2g fiber), 3g pro.

OPTIONAL STREUSEL TOPPING: Combine ½ cup sugar, ⅓ cup all-purpose flour and ½ tsp. ground cinnamon; cut in ¼ cup cold butter until crumbly. Before baking, sprinkle over filled muffin cups; bake as directed.

Strawberries & Cream Bread

Once strawberry-picking time arrives each summer, my husband and I look forward to this bread. Since only fresh strawberries will do, I have been thinking of trying a different kind of berry so we can enjoy it more often.
—*Suzanne Randall, Dexter, ME*

PREP: 15 MIN. • BAKE: 65 MIN. + COOLING • MAKES: 1 LOAF (12 SLICES)

½ cup butter, softened
¾ cup sugar
2 large eggs, room temperature
½ cup sour cream
1 tsp. vanilla extract
1¾ cups all-purpose flour
½ tsp. baking powder
½ tsp. baking soda
½ tsp. salt
¼ tsp. ground cinnamon
¾ cup chopped fresh strawberries
¾ cup chopped walnuts, toasted, divided

1. Preheat oven to 350°. In a large bowl, cream butter and sugar until light and fluffy, 5-7 minutes. Beat in eggs. Add sour cream and vanilla; mix well.

2. In another bowl, whisk flour, baking powder, baking soda, salt and cinnamon; gradually stir into creamed mixture just until moistened. Fold in strawberries and ½ cup nuts.

3. Pour into a greased 8x4-in. loaf pan. Sprinkle with the remaining nuts. Bake 65-70 minutes or until a toothpick inserted in center comes out clean. Cool in pan 10 minutes before removing to a wire rack to cool completely.

1 SLICE: 199 cal., 11g fat (5g sat. fat), 47mg chol., 196mg sod., 21g carb. (10g sugars, 1g fiber), 4g pro.

Banana Berry Muffins

My original version of this recipe called for Raisin Bran, but one day
I used bran flakes with added blueberries because it was what I had on hand.
I liked the muffins better, so now I always make them this way.
—*Alyce Wyman, Pembina, ND*

PREP: 20 MIN. • **BAKE:** 20 MIN./BATCH • **MAKES:** 1½ DOZEN

4 cups bran flakes
½ cup buttermilk
½ cup butter, softened
1 cup sugar
2 large eggs, room
   temperature
1½ cups mashed ripe
   bananas (about
   3 medium)
1 tsp. vanilla extract
1½ cups all-purpose flour
1½ tsp. baking powder
½ tsp. salt
¼ tsp. baking soda
1 cup fresh or frozen
   blueberries
⅓ cup finely chopped
   pecans
⅓ cup packed brown
   sugar
¾ tsp. ground cinnamon

1. Preheat oven to 350°. In a large bowl, combine bran flakes and buttermilk; set aside.

2. In another large bowl, cream butter and sugar until light and fluffy, 5-7 minutes. Beat in eggs, 1 at a time, beating well after each addition. Beat in bananas and vanilla (mixture will appear curdled).

3. Combine the flour, baking powder, salt and baking soda; gradually stir into the creamed mixture just until moistened. Stir in bran mixture. Fold in blueberries. Fill greased or paper-lined muffin cups three-fourths full.

4. Combine the pecans, brown sugar and cinnamon; sprinkle over batter. Bake for 20-25 minutes or until a toothpick inserted in center comes out clean. Cool for 5 minutes before removing from pans to wire racks. Serve warm.

FREEZE OPTION: Freeze cooled muffins in airtight freezer containers. To use, thaw at room temperature or, if desired, microwave each muffin on high for 20-30 minutes or until heated through.

1 MUFFIN: 218 cal., 8g fat (4g sat. fat), 38mg chol., 249mg sod., 37g carb. (21g sugars, 3g fiber), 3g pro.

Yummy Apricot Pecan Bread

Every time I prepare this yummy bread, I always receive raves. It's perfect with coffee or as a gift, plus it's really quick and easy to prepare.
—Joan Hallford, North Richland Hills, TX

PREP: 20 MIN. • BAKE: 40 MIN. + COOLING • MAKES: 2 LOAVES

2½ cups all-purpose flour
¾ cup sugar
2 tsp. baking soda
1 tsp. ground cinnamon
¼ tsp. salt
¼ tsp. ground nutmeg
1 cup 2% milk
2 large eggs, room temperature
⅓ cup butter, melted
2 cups shredded cheddar cheese
1 cup finely chopped dried apricots
¾ cup finely chopped pecans

TOPPING
3 Tbsp. packed brown sugar
1 Tbsp. butter
½ tsp. ground cinnamon

1. Preheat oven to 350°. In a large bowl, combine the first 6 ingredients. In a small bowl, beat the milk, eggs and butter; stir into dry ingredients just until moistened. Fold in the cheese, apricots and pecans.

2. Spoon batter into 2 greased 8x4-in. loaf pans. Combine the topping ingredients; sprinkle over batter.

3. Bake for 40-45 minutes or until a toothpick inserted in center comes out clean. Cool loaves for 10 minutes before removing from pans to wire racks.

FREEZE OPTION: Securely wrap and freeze individual cooled loaves. To use, thaw at room temperature

1 SLICE: 189 cal., 9g fat (4g sat. fat), 36mg chol., 223mg sod., 23g carb. (11g sugars, 1g fiber), 5g pro.

NOTES

CHAPTER 4
Breads Made Easy

Italian Herb & Cheese Breadsticks

Thanks to frozen bread dough, these breadsticks are not only ultra cheesy but ultra easy! The delectable bites are perfect to dip into warm marinara sauce.
—*Rebekah Beyer, Sabetha, KS*

PREP: 20 MIN. + RISING • **BAKE:** 20 MIN. • **MAKES:** 2 DOZEN

1 loaf (1 lb.) frozen bread dough, thawed
⅓ cup butter, softened
1 Tbsp. Italian seasoning
1 garlic clove, minced
¾ cup shredded part-skim mozzarella cheese
½ cup grated Parmesan cheese, divided
    Marinara sauce, warmed, optional

1. On a lightly floured surface, roll dough into a 12-in. square. In a small bowl, mix butter, Italian seasoning and garlic; spread over dough. Sprinkle mozzarella cheese and ¼ cup Parmesan cheese over the butter mixture. Fold dough in thirds over filling; pinch seams to seal.

2. Cut crosswise into twenty-four ½-in.-wide strips. Twist each strip 2 or 3 times. Place twists 2 in. apart on greased baking sheets. Cover and let rise until almost doubled, about 30 minutes.

3. Preheat oven to 375°. Sprinkle with the remaining Parmesan cheese. Bake 20-22 minutes or until golden brown. If desired, serve with marinara sauce.

1 BREADSTICK: 93 cal., 4g fat (2g sat. fat), 10mg chol., 180mg sod., 10g carb. (1g sugars, 1g fiber), 3g pro.

Sweet Onion Bread Skillet

Because there are just a few ingredients in this recipe, you'll get the best results if you use the finest-quality foods, like a fresh Vidalia onion and aged Parmesan cheese.
—*Lisa Speer, Palm Beach, FL*

PREP: 25 MIN. • **BAKE:** 10 MIN. • **MAKES:** 4 SERVINGS

1 **large sweet onion, thinly sliced**
2 **Tbsp. butter**
2 **Tbsp. olive oil, divided**
1 **can (13.8 oz.) refrigerated pizza crust**
¼ **cup grated Parmesan cheese**

READER REVIEW

"I had leftover beer bread so I followed the instructions for the topping and did not use the pizza crust. It was excellent! My husband is not the biggest fan of onions but he dubbed this a keeper."

—EJSHELLABARGER, TASTEOFHOME.COM

1. Preheat oven to 450°. In a large cast-iron or other ovenproof skillet, saute onion in butter and 1 Tbsp. oil until softened. Reduce heat to medium-low; cook, stirring occasionally, until golden brown, 15-20 minutes. Remove onions from skillet and set aside.

2. Brush bottom and sides of skillet with the remaining oil. Unroll crust into skillet; flatten crust and build up edge slightly. Top with the onion mixture and cheese. Bake until golden brown, 10-12 minutes. Cut into 4 wedges.

1 WEDGE: 415 cal., 17g fat (5g sat. fat), 19mg chol., 776mg sod., 53g carb. (9g sugars, 2g fiber), 11g pro.

Green Onion Rolls

These savory, elegant rolls make a great party appetizer as well as a delicious accompaniment to a sit-down meal. Better double the batch—these rolls always disappear fast!
—*Jane Kroeger, Key Largo, FL*

PREP: 30 MIN. + RISING • **BAKE:** 20 MIN. • **MAKES:** 1 DOZEN

1 Tbsp. butter
1½ cups chopped green onions
½ tsp. pepper
¾ tsp. garlic salt, optional
1 loaf (1 lb.) frozen bread dough, thawed
½ cup shredded part-skim mozzarella cheese
⅓ cup grated Parmesan cheese

1. In a large skillet, heat butter over medium-high heat; saute green onions until tender. Stir in pepper and, if desired, garlic salt. Remove from heat.

2. On a lightly floured surface, roll dough into a 12x8-in. rectangle. Spread with the onion mixture. Sprinkle with the cheeses.

3. Roll up dough jelly-roll style, starting with a long side; pinch seam to seal. Cut into 12 slices; place in greased muffin cups. Cover; let rise in a warm place until doubled, about 30 minutes. Preheat oven to 375°.

4. Bake until golden brown, 18-20 minutes. Remove from pan to a wire rack. Serve warm.

1 ROLL: 142 cal., 4g fat (1g sat. fat), 7mg chol., 415mg sod., 20g carb. (2g sugars, 2g fiber), 6g pro.

Gooey Old-Fashioned Steamed Molasses Bread

When I was growing up, the smell of this bread greeted me as I walked in the door from school. I thought everyone baked bread in a slow cooker! My grandmother, my mother and I—and now my daughters—all make this. It's comfort food at its best!
—*Bonnie Geavaras, Chandler, AZ*

PREP: 20 MIN. • **COOK:** 3 HOURS + COOLING • **MAKES:** 16 SERVINGS

2 cups all-bran
1 cup all-purpose flour
1 cup whole wheat flour
1 cup dried cranberries
1½ tsp. baking powder
1 tsp. baking soda
1 tsp. salt
½ tsp. ground cinnamon
1 large egg, room temperature
1¾ cups buttermilk
½ cup molasses
2 Tbsp. honey

1. Layer two 24-in. pieces of foil. Starting with a long side, roll up foil to make a 1-in.-wide strip; shape into a coil. Place on bottom of a 5-qt. slow cooker to make a rack.

2. Combine all-bran, flours, cranberries, baking powder, baking soda, salt and cinnamon. In another bowl, beat the egg, buttermilk, molasses and honey. Stir into the flour mixture just until blended (do not overbeat).

3. Pour batter into a greased and floured 2-qt. baking dish. Tightly cover with lightly greased foil. Place in prepared slow cooker. Cook, covered, on high about 3 hours, until a thermometer reads 190-200°.

4. Remove dish to a wire rack; cool 10 minutes before inverting loaf onto the rack. Serve warm or cold.

1 WEDGE: 157 cal., 1g fat (0 sat. fat), 13mg chol., 351mg sod., 36g carb. (19g sugars, 4g fiber), 4g pro.

Cranberry Brie Pecan Pinwheels

This recipe is a twist on baked Brie. My family always requests these during the holidays. The creamy, tart pastries are delicious and make the kitchen smell amazing!
—*Jacquie Franklin, Hot Springs, MT*

PREP: 20 MIN. • **BAKE:** 15 MIN. • **MAKES:** ABOUT 2 DOZEN

1 lb. Brie cheese, rind removed
1 pkg. (17.3 oz.) frozen puff pastry, thawed
⅔ cup whole-berry cranberry sauce
1 large egg
1 Tbsp. water
½ cup chopped pecans

1. Preheat oven to 400°. Beat trimmed Brie on medium until smooth and creamy, about 5 minutes.

2. On a lightly floured surface, unfold 1 sheet puff pastry; spread half the Brie to within ½ in. of edges. Spread half the cranberry sauce over the Brie. Starting with a short side, roll up jelly-roll style. Cut crosswise into 12 slices.

3. Place pastries on parchment-lined baking sheets. Whisk egg with water; brush over slices. Sprinkle with chopped pecans. Repeat with remaining puff pastry. Bake until golden brown, 15-20 minutes.

1 PASTRY: 193 cal., 13g fat (5g sat. fat), 27mg chol., 193mg sod., 15g carb. (2g sugars, 2g fiber), 6g pro.

Campfire Cinnamon Twists

Cinnamon rolls get the toasty treatment when wrapped around skewers and warmed over a fire. Brush with butter, then sprinkle with sugar and spice.

—Lauren McAnelly, Des Moines, IA

TAKES: 25 MIN. • MAKES: 16 SERVINGS

¼ cup sugar
2 tsp. ground cinnamon
1 tube (12.4 oz.) refrigerated cinnamon rolls with icing
2 Tbsp. butter, melted

1. Mix sugar and cinnamon. Remove icing from cinnamon rolls; transfer to a resealable plastic bag for drizzling.

2. Separate rolls; cut each in half. Roll halves into 6-in. ropes. Wrap each rope tightly around a long metal skewer, beginning ½ in. from the pointed end; pinch each end of the rope to secure it to the skewer.

3. Cook the rolls over a hot campfire until golden brown, about 5 minutes, turning occasionally. Brush with butter; sprinkle with sugar mixture. Cut a small hole in 1 corner of icing bag. Drizzle icing over twists.

1 TWIST: 98 cal., 4g fat (2g sat. fat), 4mg chol., 183mg sod., 15g carb. (8g sugars, 0 fiber), 1g pro.

NOTES

_____
_____
_____
_____
_____
_____
_____
_____
_____
_____

Garlic & Cheese Flatbread

Unless you plan to make two of these, don't count on leftovers!
As an appetizer or side, this cheesy flatbread will be devoured
in less time than it takes to bake. And that's not long!
—*Suzanne Zick, Maiden, NC*

TAKES: 25 MIN. • MAKES: 12 SERVINGS

1 tube (11 oz.) refrigerated thin pizza crust
2 Tbsp. butter, melted
1 Tbsp. minced fresh basil
4 garlic cloves, minced
¾ cup shredded cheddar cheese
½ cup grated Romano cheese
¼ cup grated Parmesan cheese

1. Preheat oven to 425°. Unroll the dough into a greased 15x10x1-in. baking pan; flatten dough to 13x9-in. rectangle and build up the edges slightly.

2. Drizzle dough with melted butter. Sprinkle with basil, garlic and cheeses.

3. Bake at 425° until crisp, 11-14 minutes. Cut into squares; serve warm.

1 PIECE: 146 cal., 8g fat (4g sat. fat), 19mg chol., 317mg sod., 13g carb. (1g sugars, 0 fiber), 6g pro.

READER REVIEW

"I didn't have pizza crust on hand so I used a tube of crescent rolls instead. I just made sure all the seams were sealed and did the rest as it called for, then baked at 375° for about 8 minutes. It was so very tasty and my family loved it!"

– BUTTERFLY3GAYLE, TASTEOFHOME.COM

Bacon-Wrapped Breadsticks

I first tried these at a restaurant and the owner was kind enough
to share the recipe. I used refrigerated dough, and the first time I made
this for my family, not a crumb was left and everyone was asking for more!
—*Wendy Domres, West Bend, WI*

TAKES: 30 MIN. • **MAKES:** 2 DOZEN

24 bacon strips
 2 tubes (11 oz. each)
    refrigerated
    breadsticks
 1 cup grated Parmesan
    cheese
 2 tsp. garlic powder

1. Preheat oven to 375°. Wrap a bacon strip around each breadstick; place on baking sheets. Bake for 15-20 minutes or until golden brown.

2. In a shallow bowl, combine cheese and garlic powder. Roll warm breadsticks in the cheese mixture.

1 BREADSTICK: 189 cal., 12g fat (5g sat. fat), 18mg chol., 425mg sod., 13g carb. (2g sugars, 0 fiber), 6g pro.

Quick Focaccia Bread

Green olives complement my speedy version of the beloved
Italian bread. Try this focaccia with minestrone or Italian wedding soup,
or serve it with an antipasto tray for a hearty appetizer the guys will love.
—*Ivy Laffoon, Ceres, CA*

TAKES: 30 MIN. • **MAKES:** 8 SERVINGS

1 loaf (1 lb.) frozen bread
dough, thawed
½ cup sliced pimiento-
stuffed olives
½ cup shredded Colby-
Monterey Jack cheese
½ cup shredded
Parmesan cheese
1 tsp. Italian seasoning
2 Tbsp. olive oil

1. Preheat oven to 350°. On an ungreased baking sheet, pat dough into a 12x6-in. rectangle. Build up edges slightly. Top with olives, cheeses and Italian seasoning; press gently into dough. Drizzle with oil.

2. Bake until cheese is melted and golden brown, 15-20 minutes. Let stand for 5 minutes before slicing.

1 SLICE: 249 cal., 11g fat (3g sat. fat), 10mg chol., 623mg sod., 31g carb. (2g sugars, 2g fiber), 9g pro.

READER REVIEW
"I made this to go alongside shrimp scampi over angel hair pasta. My daughter and I loved it. I didn't have grated cojack cheese so I substituted what I did have—sharp cheddar, a little bit of Gouda and some mozzarella. Next time I'll try pressing out the dough to fill a 15x10x1-in. rimmed baking pan, because I like my focaccia on the thinner side. This is a great, versatile recipe."
—AQUARELLE, TASTEOFHOME.COM

Berry-Filled Doughnuts

Four ingredients are all you'll need for this sure-to-be-popular treat. Friends and family will never guess that refrigerated buttermilk biscuits are the base for these golden, jelly-filled doughnuts.
—*Ginny Watson, Broken Arrow, OK*

TAKES: 25 MIN. • MAKES: 10 DOUGHNUTS

Oil for deep-fat frying
2 **tubes (6 oz. each) small refrigerated flaky biscuits (5 count)**
½ **cup seedless strawberry jam**
¾ **cup confectioners' sugar**

1. In an electric skillet or deep fryer, heat oil to 350°. Separate biscuits; press each to flatten slightly. Fry biscuits, a few at a time, until golden brown, 1-1¼ minutes per side. Drain on paper towels.

2. Cut a small hole in the tip of a pastry bag; insert a small pastry tip. Fill bag with jam. With a small knife, pierce a hole into the side of each doughnut; fill with jam.

3. Toss with confectioners' sugar. Serve warm.

1 DOUGHNUT: 190 cal., 7g fat (1g sat. fat), 0 chol., 360mg sod., 30g carb. (17g sugars, 0 fiber), 2g pro.

Brie & Caramelized Onion Flatbread

This classy flatbread makes a great party appetizer. Saute the onions and garlic
a day ahead so it's easy to put together on the day of the event.
Prepared pizza dough makes it a snap.
—*Trisha Kruse, Eagle, ID*

PREP: 45 MIN. • **BAKE:** 20 MIN. + STANDING • **MAKES:** 1 FLATBREAD (12 PIECES)

2 Tbsp. butter
3 large sweet onions, halved and thinly sliced (about 6 cups)
2 garlic cloves, minced
1 Tbsp. brown sugar
1 Tbsp. balsamic vinegar
½ tsp. salt
¼ tsp. pepper
1 loaf (1 lb.) frozen pizza dough, thawed
8 oz. Brie cheese, cut into ½-in. pieces

1. Preheat oven to 425°. Grease a 15x10x1-in. baking pan; set aside. In a large skillet, heat butter over medium heat. Add onions; cook and stir 4-6 minutes or until softened. Reduce heat to medium-low; cook 25-30 minutes or until deep golden brown, stirring occasionally. Add garlic; cook and stir 1 minute longer.

2. Add brown sugar, vinegar, salt and pepper to onion mixture. Cook and stir 5 minutes longer. Press dough into a 12x10-in. rectangle onto prepared pan. Top with onion mixture and cheese. Bake 20-25 minutes or until golden brown. Let stand 10 minutes before cutting.

1 PIECE: 206 cal., 9g fat (5g sat. fat), 24mg chol., 333mg sod., 25g carb. (6g sugars, 1g fiber), 8g pro.

Monkey Bread

Both of my boys really enjoyed helping me make monkey bread when they were young. It seemed to taste twice as good when they helped fix it. It's one of our favorites for breakfast or as a snack.
—*Carol Allen, McLeansboro, IL*

PREP: 15 MIN. • **BAKE:** 30 MIN. + COOLING • **MAKES:** 12 SERVINGS

1 pkg. (3½ oz.) cook-and-serve butterscotch pudding mix
¾ cup sugar
3 tsp. ground cinnamon
½ cup finely chopped pecans, optional
½ cup butter, melted
3 tubes (10 oz. each) refrigerated biscuits

1. Preheat oven to 350°. Grease a 10-in. fluted tube pan; set aside. Combine pudding mix, sugar, cinnamon and, if desired, pecans. Pour butter into a shallow bowl; quarter biscuits. Dip several pieces into butter; place in pudding mixture and toss to coat. Arrange biscuit pieces in the prepared pan.

2. Repeat until all biscuit pieces are dipped. coated and arranged in the pan. Bake until browned, 30-35 minutes. Cool 5-10 minutes before inverting onto a serving plate.

1 SERVING: 223 cal., 11g fat (5g sat. fat), 20mg chol., 343mg sod., 30g carb. (19g sugars, 1g fiber), 2g pro.

How To Make Monkey Bread

1. Use a spoon to dip the biscuit pieces in the butter. You don't need to soak them—a quick dip will do.

2. Place the wet biscuit pieces in the dry mix and toss to coat. Working with 4-5 pieces at a time gives you room for tossing and allows the pieces to be coated evenly.

3. As you place the pieces in the pan, they don't have to be neatly layered; try to fill gaps as you go. Then dip, coat and arrange another batch of biscuit pieces.

4. Letting the baked bread cool for 5-10 minutes before inverting lets it release from the pan so it won't tear.

Swiss Cheese Bread

This bread will receive rave reviews, whether you serve it as an appetizer or with a meal. For real convenience, you can assemble it ahead of time and freeze it!
—Karla Boice, Mahtomedi, MN

TAKES: 30 MIN. • **MAKES:** 20 SERVINGS

1 **loaf (18-20 in.) French bread**
1 **cup butter, softened**
2 **cups shredded Swiss cheese**
¾ **tsp. celery seed**
¾ **tsp. garlic powder**
3 **Tbsp. dried parsley flakes**

1. Preheat oven to 425°. Cut bread in half crosswise. Make diagonal cuts, 1 in. apart, through bread but not through the bottom.

2. Combine all the remaining ingredients. Spread half the butter mixture between bread slices. Spread the remaining mixture over top and sides of bread.

3. Place bread on double thickness of foil; cover loosely with more foil. Bake for 20-30 minutes. For last 5 minutes, remove the foil covering the bread to allow it to brown.

1 SLICE: 187 cal., 13g fat (8g sat. fat), 34mg chol., 231mg sod., 12g carb. (1g sugars, 1g fiber), 6g pro.

NOTES

Pesto Pull-Apart Bread

I combined some of my favorite flavors in an easy bread to complement our Italian meals. I make the pesto, oven-dried tomatoes and roasted red peppers, but store-bought versions will work just as well.
—*Sue Gronholz, Beaver Dam, WI*

PREP: 10 MIN. • **BAKE:** 30 MIN. • **MAKES:** 16 SERVINGS

1 tube (16.3 oz.) large refrigerated buttermilk biscuits
¼ cup olive oil
2 Tbsp. prepared pesto
¼ cup sun-dried tomatoes (not packed in oil)
¼ cup roasted sweet red peppers, drained and diced
¼ cup sliced ripe olives
1 cup shredded mozzarella and provolone cheese blend
   Additional prepared pesto, optional

1. Preheat oven to 350°. Cut each biscuit into 4 pieces. Combine olive oil and pesto. Dip biscuit pieces into the pesto mixture until coated; place in an 8-in. round baking pan. Top with sun-dried tomatoes, roasted red peppers and ripe olives.

2. Bake until golden brown, about 25 minutes. Sprinkle with cheese; return to oven, and bake until melted, about 5 minutes longer. Cut into wedges or pull apart; serve warm, with additional pesto if desired.

1 SERVING: 152 cal., 9g fat (3g sat. fat), 5mg chol., 410mg sod., 13g carb. (2g sugars, 1g fiber), 3g pro.

Swiss-Onion Bread Ring

With the ease of refrigerated bread dough, this tempting cheesy bread
has delicious down-home goodness. You'll find it crisp and
golden on the outside, rich and buttery inside.

—Judi Messina, Coeur d'Alene, ID

PREP: 10 MIN. • **BAKE:** 25 MIN. • **MAKES:** 1 LOAF (12 SERVINGS)

2½ tsp. poppy seeds,
    divided
2 tubes (11 oz. each)
    refrigerated French
    bread dough
1 cup shredded Swiss
    cheese
¾ cup sliced green onions
6 Tbsp. butter, melted

1. Preheat oven to 375°. Grease a 10-in. fluted tube pan,
and then sprinkle with ½ tsp. poppy seeds. Cut dough into
forty 1-in. pieces; place half in the prepared pan. Sprinkle
with half of the cheese and onions. Top with 1 tsp. poppy
seeds; drizzle with half of the butter. Repeat layers.

2. Bake for 30-35 minutes or until golden brown.
Immediately invert onto a wire rack. Serve warm.

1 PIECE: 152 cal., 9g fat (6g sat. fat), 24mg chol., 246mg sod.,
12g carb. (2g sugars, 1g fiber), 5g pro.

FILLING THE FLUTES
When greasing a fluted
tube pan, it's best to
use a bit of shortening
on a folded paper towel
to coat the cracks and
crevices—using baking
spray is quicker, but it's
easy to overdo it.

Cheddar Corn Dog Muffins

I wanted a change from hot dogs, so I made corn dog muffins. I added jalapenos to this kid-friendly recipe and that won my husband over, too.
—*Becky Tarala, Palm Coast, FL*

TAKES: 25 MIN. • MAKES: 9 MUFFINS

1 pkg. (8½ oz.) cornbread/muffin mix
⅔ cup 2% milk
1 large egg, room temperature, lightly beaten
5 turkey hot dogs, sliced
½ cup shredded sharp cheddar cheese
2 Tbsp. finely chopped pickled jalapeno, optional

1. Preheat oven to 400°. Line 9 muffin cups with foil liners or grease 9 nonstick muffin cups.

2. In a small bowl, combine muffin mix, milk and egg; stir in hot dogs, cheese and, if desired, jalapeno. Fill prepared cups three-fourths full.

3. Bake until a toothpick inserted in center comes out clean, 14-18 minutes. Cool 5 minutes before removing from pan to a wire rack. Serve warm. Refrigerate leftovers.

FREEZE OPTION: Freeze cooled muffins in freezer containers. To use, microwave each muffin on high until heated through, 30-60 seconds.

1 MUFFIN: 216 cal., 10g fat (4g sat. fat), 46mg chol., 619mg sod., 23g carb. (7g sugars, 2g fiber), 8g pro.

Mushroom Cheese Bread

This savory grilled bread is delightful with barbecued steak,
baked potatoes and corn on the cob. For a variation,
we sometimes use half cheddar cheese and half mozzarella.

—Dolly McDonald, Edmonton, AB

TAKES: 15 MIN. • **MAKES:** 12 SERVINGS

1 cup shredded part-skim mozzarella cheese
1 can (4 oz.) mushroom stems and pieces, drained
⅓ cup mayonnaise
2 Tbsp. shredded Parmesan cheese
2 Tbsp. chopped green onion
1 loaf (1 lb.) unsliced French bread

1. In a small bowl, combine the mozzarella cheese, mushrooms, mayonnaise, Parmesan cheese and onion. Cut bread in half lengthwise; spread the cheese mixture over the cut sides.

2. Grill, covered, over indirect heat or broil 4 in. from the heat until lightly browned, 5-10 minutes. Slice and serve warm.

1 SLICE: 180 cal., 8g fat (2g sat. fat), 10mg chol., 347mg sod., 20g carb. (1g sugars, 1g fiber), 6g pro.

READER REVIEW

"This is an amazing recipe. Very tasty and quick to make. We serve it often, either as an appetizer or beside a soup for supper. I usually do about 1½ times the cheese mixture as we like a lot of the gooey, bubbly warm topping. Also, it's very good with half mozzarella and half chedder instead of all mozzarella."

—DABAKER55126, TASTEOFHOME.COM

Cheesy Pizza Rolls

The cast-iron skillet browns these delicious rolls to perfection. My family can't get enough. Use whatever pizza toppings your family likes best.
—*Dorothy Smith, El Dorado, AR*

PREP: 15 MIN. • BAKE: 25 MIN. • MAKES: 8 APPETIZERS

1 loaf (1 lb.) frozen pizza dough, thawed
½ cup pasta sauce
1 cup shredded part-skim mozzarella cheese, divided
1 cup coarsely chopped pepperoni (about 64 slices)
½ lb. bulk Italian sausage, cooked and crumbled
¼ cup grated Parmesan cheese
Optional: Minced fresh basil and crushed red pepper flakes

1. Preheat oven to 400°. On a lightly floured surface, roll dough into a 16x10-in. rectangle. Brush with pasta sauce to within ½ in. of edges.

2. Sprinkle with ½ cup mozzarella cheese, the pepperoni, sausage and Parmesan. Roll up jelly-roll style, starting with a long side; pinch seam to seal. Cut into 8 slices. Place in a greased 9-in. cast-iron skillet or greased 9-in. round baking pan, cut side down.

3. Bake for 20 minutes; sprinkle with the remaining mozzarella cheese. Bake until golden brown, 5-10 minutes longer. If desired, serve with minced fresh basil and crushed red pepper flakes.

1 ROLL: 355 cal., 19g fat (7g sat. fat), 42mg chol., 978mg sod., 29g carb. (3g sugars, 0 fiber), 14g pro.

Sausage Cheese Biscuits

These biscuits are a brunch-time favorite.
I love that they don't require any special ingredients.
—*Marlene Neideigh, Myrtle Point, OR*

TAKES: 30 MIN. • MAKES: 10 SERVINGS

1 tube (12 oz.) refrigerated buttermilk biscuits (10 count)
1 pkg. (8 oz.) frozen fully cooked breakfast sausage links, thawed
2 large eggs, beaten
½ cup shredded cheddar cheese
3 Tbsp. chopped green onions

1. Preheat oven to 400°. Roll out each biscuit into a 5-in. circle; place each in an ungreased muffin cup. Cut sausages into fourths; brown in a skillet. Drain. Divide sausages among cups.

2. In a small bowl, combine eggs, cheese and onions; spoon into cups. Bake until browned, 13-15 minutes.

1 BISCUIT: 227 cal., 16g fat (6g sat. fat), 57mg chol., 548mg sod., 16g carb. (3g sugars, 0 fiber), 8g pro.

Herb Biscuit Loaf

These buttery, golden rolls are a sure way to make any meal special—from Thanksgiving dinner to a weekday supper. Their wonderful herb flavor makes my husband think I fussed.
—*Amy Smith, Maplewood, MN*

PREP: 15 MIN. • **BAKE:** 30 MIN. • **MAKES:** 10 SERVINGS

¼ cup butter, melted
½ tsp. dried minced onion
½ tsp. dried basil
¼ to ½ tsp. caraway
   seeds
⅛ tsp. garlic powder
2 tubes (12 oz. each)
   buttermilk biscuits

Preheat oven to 350°. In a shallow bowl, combine the first 5 ingredients. Dip each biscuit in the butter mixture, then fold in half; place the folded biscuits in rows in a greased 8-in. square baking pan. Drizzle with the remaining butter mixture. Bake until golden brown, 27-30 minutes.

1 PIECE: 123 cal., 5g fat (3g sat. fat), 12mg chol., 337mg sod., 16g carb. (0 sugars, 0 fiber), 3g pro.

SLOW DOWN ON SALT
Unless specially noted, *Taste of Home* recipes use lightly salted butter. If you're watching your salt, you might prefer to use unsalted for this recipe.

S'mores Monkey Bread Muffins

When it comes to mini versions of anything, I'm sold! These muffins are ooey-gooey individual-sized monkey breads made with frozen dinner rolls, graham cracker crumbs, chocolate chips and mini marshmallows. They couldn't be easier to make, and kids just love them.
—*Tina Butler, Royse City, TX*

PREP: 35 MIN. • BAKE: 15 MIN. • MAKES: 1 DOZEN

15 frozen bread dough dinner rolls, thawed but still cold
1⅓ cups graham cracker crumbs
½ cup sugar
6 Tbsp. butter, cubed
1 cup miniature semisweet chocolate chips, divided
¾ cup miniature marshmallows

ICING
1 cup confectioners' sugar
½ tsp. butter, softened
1 to 2 Tbsp. 2% milk

1. Preheat oven to 375°. Line 12 muffin cups with foil liners.

2. Using a sharp knife, cut each roll into 4 pieces. In a shallow bowl, mix cracker crumbs and sugar. In a large microwave-safe bowl, microwave butter until melted. Dip 3 pieces of dough in butter, then roll in crumb mixture to coat; place in a prepared muffin cup. Repeat until all the muffin cups are filled. Sprinkle tops with ¾ cup chocolate chips and marshmallows.

3. Toss the remaining dough pieces with remaining butter, rewarming the butter if necessary. Place 2 additional dough pieces into each cup and sprinkle with remaining chocolate chips.

4. Bake until golden brown, 15-20 minutes. Cool for 5 minutes before removing from pan to a wire rack. Mix icing ingredients; spoon over tops. Serve warm.

1 MUFFIN: 351 cal., 13g fat (6g sat. fat), 16mg chol., 337mg sod., 57g carb. (29g sugars, 3g fiber), 6g pro.

Lemon Pull-Apart Coffee Cake

I found this recipe in a newspaper and make it often. I keep a tube of
buttermilk biscuit dough on hand so I can bake it when unexpected
company stops in. We enjoy it served with hot coffee.
—*Mary Tallman, Arbor Vitae, WI*

TAKES: 30 MIN. • **MAKES:** 10 SERVINGS

¼ cup sugar
¼ cup chopped walnuts
¼ cup golden raisins
2 Tbsp. butter, melted
2 tsp. grated lemon zest
1 tube (12 oz.)
    refrigerated buttermilk
    biscuits

GLAZE
½ cup confectioners'
    sugar
1 Tbsp. lemon juice

1. Preheat oven to 375°. In a large bowl, combine the first
5 ingredients. Separate the biscuits and cut each into
quarters; toss with sugar mixture. Arrange in a greased
9-in. round baking pan.

2. Bake until golden brown, 20-25 minutes. Immediately
invert onto a wire rack. In a small bowl, mix confectioners'
sugar and lemon juice until smooth; drizzle over coffee
cake. Serve warm.

4 PIECES : 175 cal., 5g fat (2g sat. fat), 6mg chol., 315mg sod.,
31g carb. (13g sugars, 0 fiber), 4g pro.

NOTES

Overnight Cherry Danish

These rolls with their cherry-filled centers melt in
your mouth and store well, unfrosted, in the freezer.
—*Leann Sauder, Tremont, IL*

PREP: 1½ HOURS + CHILLING • **BAKE:** 15 MIN. • **MAKES:** 3 DOZEN

2 pkg. (¼ oz. each) active dry yeast
½ cup warm 2% milk (110° to 115°)
6 cups all-purpose flour
⅓ cup sugar
2 tsp. salt
1 cup cold butter, cubed
1½ cups warm half-and-half cream (70° to 80°)
6 large egg yolks, room temperature
1 can (21 oz.) cherry pie filling

ICING
3 cups confectioners' sugar
2 Tbsp. butter, softened
¼ tsp. vanilla extract
Dash salt
4 to 5 Tbsp. half-and-half cream

1. In a small bowl, dissolve yeast in warm milk. In a large bowl, combine flour, sugar and salt. Cut in butter until crumbly. Add yeast mixture, cream and egg yolks; stir until the mixture forms a soft dough (dough will be sticky). Refrigerate, covered, overnight.

2. Punch down dough. Turn onto a lightly floured surface; divide into 4 portions. Roll each portion of dough into an 18x4-in. rectangle; cut each rectangle into 4x1-in. strips.

3. Place 2 strips side by side; twist together. Shape into a ring and pinch ends together. Place 2 in. apart on greased baking sheets. Repeat with the remaining strips. Cover with kitchen towels; let rise in a warm place until doubled, about 45 minutes.

4. Preheat oven to 350°. Using the end of a wooden spoon handle, make a ½-in.-deep indentation in the center of each Danish. Fill each with about 1 Tbsp. pie filling. Bake 14-16 minutes or until lightly browned. Remove from pans to wire racks to cool.

5. For icing, in a bowl, beat confectioners' sugar, butter, vanilla, salt and enough cream to reach the desired consistency. Drizzle over Danishes.

1 DANISH: 218 cal., 8g fat (5g sat. fat), 55mg chol., 188mg sod., 33g carb. (16g sugars, 1g fiber), 3g pro.

Surprise Monkey Bread

When my neighbor hosts brunch, she always asks that I make this treat.
I also make a savory version with garlic and cheese for dinner.
This recipe also works well in a 13x9-in. pan, if you prefer.
—*Lois Rutherford, Elkton, FL*

PREP: 25 MIN. • **BAKE:** 40 MIN. • **MAKES:** 1 LOAF (12 SERVINGS)

1 cup packed brown sugar
½ cup butter, cubed
2 tubes (12 oz. each) retrigerated flaky buttermilk biscuits
½ cup sugar
1 Tbsp. ground cinnamon
8 oz. cream cheese, cut into 20 cubes
1½ cups chopped walnuts

MAKE MINE A DANISH!
Halve the amount of cream cheese and add 1 tsp. of your favorite jam to each biscuit for a fun brunch-worthy take on Danish.

1. Preheat oven to 350°. In a small microwave-safe bowl, heat brown sugar and butter on high for 1 minute or until the sugar is dissolved; set aside.

2. Flatten each biscuit into a 3-in. circle. Combine sugar and cinnamon; sprinkle ½ tsp. in the center of each biscuit. Top with a cream cheese cube. Fold dough over filling; pinch edges to seal tightly.

3. Sprinkle ½ cup chopped walnuts into a greased 10-in. fluted tube pan. Layer with half each of the biscuits, the cinnamon-sugar and the butter mixture, and ½ cup walnuts. Repeat layers.

4. Bake for 40-45 minutes or until golden brown. Immediately invert onto a serving platter. Serve warm. Refrigerate leftovers.

1 SLICE: 467 cal., 24g fat (10g sat. fat), 41mg chol., 625mg sod., 56g carb. (26g sugars, 1g fiber), 10g pro.

Pear-Berry Breakfast Tarts

When my kids were small, I could never get pancakes on the table while they were all still hot. Then I got the idea for these breakfast tarts. It's a simple recipe for any busy family.
—*Joan Elbourn, Gardner, MA*

PREP: 45 MIN. + CHILLING • **BAKE:** 20 MIN. • **MAKES:** 10 SERVINGS

½ **cup butter, softened**
1 **cup sugar, divided**
2 **large eggs, room temperature**
2½ **cups all-purpose flour**
2 **tsp. baking powder**
2 **cups chopped peeled pears (about 2 large)**
2 **Tbsp. cornstarch**
2 **Tbsp. water**
½ **cup fresh raspberries**
1 **large egg white**
3 **to 5 Tbsp. 2% milk, divided**

ICING
1⅓ **cups confectioners' sugar**
Food coloring, optional

1. Cream the butter and ½ cup sugar until light and fluffy, 5-7 minutes. Add eggs, 1 at a time, beating well after each addition. In another bowl, whisk flour and baking powder; gradually beat into the creamed mixture to form a dough. Divide dough in half; shape each into a rectangle. Wrap and refrigerate for 1 hour.

2. Meanwhile, in a small saucepan over medium heat, combine pears and the remaining sugar. Cook and stir until sugar is dissolved and the pears are softened, 6-8 minutes. In a small bowl, mix cornstarch and water until smooth; stir into the pear mixture. Return to a boil, stirring constantly; cook and stir 1-2 minutes or until thickened. Remove from heat; cool. Stir in raspberries.

3. Preheat oven to 350°. On a lightly floured surface, roll half the dough into a 15x8-in. rectangle. Cut into ten 4x3-in. rectangles. Transfer to parchment-lined baking sheets; spoon about 2 Tbsp. filling over each pastry to within ½ in. of edges. Roll the remaining dough into a 15x8-in. rectangle; cut into ten 4x3-in. rectangles and place over filling. Press edges with a fork to seal. Whisk egg white and 1 Tbsp. milk; brush over pastries. Bake until golden brown and filling is bubbly, 20-25 minutes.

4. Remove from baking sheets to wire racks to cool. For icing, mix confectioners' sugar and enough of remaining milk to reach desired consistency; tint with food coloring if desired. Spread or drizzle on pastries.

1 TART: 379 cal., 11g fat (6g sat. fat), 62mg chol., 193mg sod., 67g carb. (39g sugars, 2g fiber), 5g pro.

Pull-Apart Bacon Bread

I stumbled across this recipe while looking for something different to take to a brunch. Boy, am I glad I did! Everyone asked for the recipe and was surprised it only called for five ingredients. It's the perfect treat to bake for an informal get-together.
—*Traci Collins, Cheyenne, WY*

PREP: 20 MIN. + RISING • **BAKE:** 55 MIN. • **MAKES:** 16 SERVINGS

12 bacon strips, diced
1 loaf (1 lb.) frozen bread dough, thawed
2 Tbsp. olive oil, divided
1 cup shredded part skim mozzarella cheese
1 envelope (1 oz.) ranch salad dressing mix

1. In a large skillet, cook the bacon over medium heat for 5 minutes or until partially cooked; drain on paper towels. Roll out dough to ½-in. thickness; brush with 1 Tbsp. of oil. Cut into 1-in. pieces; place in a large bowl. Add the bacon, cheese, dressing mix and remaining oil; toss to coat.

2. Arrange pieces in a 9x5-in. oval on a parchment-lined baking sheet, layering as needed. Cover and let rise in a warm place for 30 minutes or until doubled.

3. Bake at 350° for 40 minutes. Cover with foil; bake 15 minutes longer or until golden brown.

1 SERVING: 149 cal., 6g fat (2g sat. fat), 8mg chol., 621mg sod., 17g carb. (1g sugars, 1g fiber), 6g pro.

NOTES

Jalapeno Cornbread Filled with Blueberry Quick Jam

Fresh jalapenos and blueberry quick jam make the perfect blend of sweet and spicy in this special cornbread. Once you eat one piece, you won't be able to resist going back for another.
—*Colleen Delawder, Herndon, VA*

PREP: 20 MIN. + CHILLING • **BAKE:** 30 MIN. + COOLING • **MAKES:** 12 SERVINGS

2 cups fresh blueberries
1 cup sugar
1 Tbsp. cider vinegar
¼ tsp. kosher salt

CORNBREAD
½ cup 2% milk
1 Tbsp. lemon juice
1½ cups all-purpose flour
½ cup yellow cornmeal
½ cup sugar
3 tsp. baking powder
½ tsp. kosher salt
2 Tbsp. unsalted butter
1 Tbsp. honey
2 large eggs, room temperature
⅓ cup canola oil
2 jalapeno peppers, seeded and minced

1. In a large heavy saucepan, combine blueberries, sugar, vinegar and kosher salt. Bring to a boil over high heat. Cook, stirring constantly, 5 minutes. Cool completely. Refrigerate, covered, overnight.

2. For cornbread, preheat oven to 350°. Combine milk and lemon juice; let stand briefly. In another bowl, whisk together flour, cornmeal, sugar, baking powder and kosher salt. In another small bowl, microwave butter and honey on high for 30 seconds; cool slightly.

3. Whisk eggs and oil into the milk mixture (mixture may appear curdled). Add the butter mixture; whisk until well combined. Add flour mixture; whisk just until combined. Fold in the jalapenos.

4. Pour 2 cups of batter into a well-buttered 10-in. fluted tube pan. Spoon half to three-fourths of the blueberry quick jam over the batter. Cover with the remaining cornbread batter. Bake until a toothpick inserted in the center comes out clean, 30-35 minutes. Cool in pan for 10 minutes; invert onto a cake plate or serving platter. Drizzle with the remaining blueberry quick jam.

1 SLICE: 289 cal., 10g fat (2g sat. fat), 37mg chol., 258mg sod., 48g carb. (30g sugars, 1g fiber), 4g pro.

Oma's Marzipan Stollen

My German grandma made this stollen for us when we were young.
I love its homey taste and how it reminds me of her and the food she made.
I often freeze this sweet bread once it's shaped into a braid—then I can pull it
out the night before, let it rise on the counter overnight, and bake it in the morning.
—*Abigail Leszczynski, Beaufort, SC*

PREP: 30 MIN. + RISING • **BAKE:** 30 MIN. • **MAKES:** 1 LOAF (16 SLICES)

3 to 3½ cups all-purpose
  flour
⅓ cup sugar
1 pkg. (¼ oz.) active dry
  yeast
1¼ cups 2% milk
6 Tbsp. butter, cubed
2 tsp. grated lemon zest

FILLING
1 can (12½ oz.) almond
  cake and pastry filling
1 cup finely ground
  almonds
1 Tbsp. 2% milk
1 tsp. rum extract

GLAZE
¼ cup confectioners'
  sugar
½ to 1 tsp. 2% milk

1. In a large bowl, combine 2 cups flour, the sugar and yeast. In a small saucepan, heat milk and butter to 120°-130°. Add to the dry ingredients; beat just until moistened. Add lemon zest; beat until smooth. Stir in enough remaining flour to form a soft dough (dough will be sticky).

2. Turn dough onto a floured surface; knead until smooth and elastic, 6-8 minutes. Place in a greased bowl, turning once to grease the top. Cover and let rise in a warm place until doubled, about 1 hour.

3. For filling, in a large bowl, beat almond pastry filling, almonds, milk and extract. Punch dough down; turn onto a floured surface. Divide into thirds. Roll each portion into a 15x6-in. rectangle. Spread each portion with a third of the filling to within ¼ in. of edges. Roll up jelly-roll style, starting with a long slide; pinch seam to seal. Place ropes on a parchment-lined baking sheet. Using a sharp knife, make a ½-in.-deep cut lengthwise down the center of each rope, stopping ½ in. from ends. Keeping the cut surfaces facing up, braid ropes. Pinch ends to seal; tuck under.

4. Cover with a kitchen towel; let rise in a warm place until almost doubled, about 30 minutes. Bake at 375° until golden brown, 30-35 minutes. Remove to a wire rack to cool. Combine glaze ingredients to desired consistency; drizzle over warm stollen.

1 SLICE: 270 cal., 10g fat (4g sat. fat), 13mg chol., 73mg sod., 41g carb. (16g sugars, 2g fiber), 5g pro.

Apple Pull-Apart Bread

Drizzled with icing, each finger-licking piece of this bread has a yummy filling of apples and pecans. The recipe is well worth the bit of extra effort.
—Carolyn Gregory, Hendersonville, TN

PREP: 40 MIN. + RISING • **BAKE:** 35 MIN. + COOLING • **MAKES:** 16 SERVINGS

1 **pkg. (¼ oz.) active dry yeast**
1 **cup warm 2% milk**
½ **cup butter, melted, divided**
1 **large egg, room temperature**
⅔ **cup plus 2 Tbsp. sugar, divided**
1 **tsp. salt**
3 **to 3½ cups all-purpose flour**
1 **medium tart apple, peeled and chopped**
½ **cup finely chopped pecans**
½ **tsp. ground cinnamon**

ICING
1 **cup confectioners' sugar**
3 **to 4½ tsp. hot water**
½ **tsp. vanilla extract**

1. In a large bowl, dissolve yeast in milk. Add 2 Tbsp. butter, egg, 2 Tbsp. sugar, the salt and 3 cups flour; beat until smooth. Add enough of the remaining flour to form a stiff dough. Turn onto a floured surface; knead until smooth and elastic, 6-8 minutes. Place in a greased bowl, turning once to grease top. Cover and let rise in a warm place until doubled, about 1 hour.

2. Combine the apple, pecans, cinnamon and the remaining sugar; set aside. Punch dough down; divide in half. Cut each half into 16 pieces. On a lightly floured surface, pat or roll out each piece into a 2½-in. circle. Place 1 tsp. of the apple mixture in the center of a circle; pinch edges together and seal, forming a ball. Dip in remaining butter. Repeat to fill, seal and dip the remaining dough pieces.

3. Place 16 balls, seam side down, in a greased 10-in. tube pan; sprinkle with ¼ cup apple mixture. Layer remaining balls; sprinkle with remaining apple mixture. Cover and let rise until nearly doubled, about 45 minutes.

4. Bake at 350° for 35-40 minutes or until golden brown. Cool for 10 minutes; remove from pan to a wire rack. Combine icing ingredients; drizzle over warm bread.

1 SERVING: 248 cal., 9g fat (4g sat. fat), 31mg chol., 218mg sod., 38g carb. (19g sugars, 1g fiber), 4g pro.

Honey-Nut Swirls

Puff pastry creates a quick and easy dough for pretty pinwheels featuring two types of nuts. The flaky treats are hard to resist.
—*Sally Sibthorpe, Shelby Township, MI*

PREP: 25 MIN. • **BAKE:** 10 MIN. • **MAKES:** 2 DOZEN

1 sheet frozen puff pastry, thawed
1 cup finely chopped walnuts
1 cup finely chopped pistachios
3 Tbsp. brown sugar
2 Tbsp. butter, softened
2 Tbsp. honey
1 tsp. ground cinnamon
¼ tsp. salt
2 Tbsp. heavy whipping cream
2 Tbsp. turbinado (washed raw) sugar or granulated sugar

1. Preheat oven to 375°. On a lightly floured surface, unfold puff pastry. Roll into a 12x9-in. rectangle.

2. In a small bowl, combine walnuts, pistachios, brown sugar, butter, honey, cinnamon and salt. Spread over the pastry to within ½ in. of edges. Roll up jelly-roll style, starting with a long side. Cut into ½-in. slices.

3. Place slices 2 in. apart on parchment-lined baking sheets. Brush with cream and sprinkle with sugar. Bake for 10-12 minutes or until lightly browned. Remove to wire racks.

1 PIECE: 141 cal., 10g fat (2g sat. fat), 4mg chol., 88mg sod., 12g carb. (5g sugars, 2g fiber), 3g pro.

Bourbon-Soaked Bacon & Ginger Cinnamon Rolls

This recipe is the perfect combination of savory and sweet. The bourbon-soaked bacon adds a smoky, savory and bold taste to normal cinnamon rolls. The ginger and pecan topping makes for a crunchy, spicy finish.
—*Shannen Casey, Citrus Heights, CA*

PREP: 25 MIN. + MARINATING • **BAKE:** 10 MIN. • **MAKES:** 8 ROLLS

8 bacon strips
¾ cup bourbon
1 tube (12.4 oz.) refrigerated cinnamon rolls with icing
½ cup chopped pecans
2 Tbsp. maple syrup
1 tsp. minced fresh gingerroot

1. Place bacon in a shallow dish; add bourbon. Cover tightly and refrigerate overnight. Remove bacon and pat dry; discard bourbon.

2. In a large skillet, cook the bacon in batches over medium heat until nearly crisp but still pliable. Remove to paper towels to drain. Discard all but 1 tsp. of the drippings.

3. Preheat oven to 375°. Separate dough into 8 rolls, reserving icing packet. Unroll spiral rolls into long strips; pat dough to form 6x1-in. strips. Place 1 bacon strip on each strip of dough, trimming bacon as needed, then reroll, forming a spiral. Pinch ends to seal. Repeat with the remaining dough. Transfer to a parchment-lined baking sheet; bake until golden brown, 9-11 minutes.

4. Meanwhile, combine pecans and maple syrup. In another bowl, stir together ginger with contents of the icing packet. In same skillet, heat the reserved bacon drippings over medium heat. Add pecans; cook, stirring frequently, until lightly toasted, 2-3 minutes.

5. Drizzle icing over warm cinnamon rolls; top with pecans.

1 ROLL: 267 cal., 14g fat (3g sat. fat), 9mg chol., 490mg sod., 28g carb. (13g sugars, 1g fiber), 5g pro.

Savory Party Bread

It's impossible to stop nibbling on warm pieces of this
cheesy, oniony loaf. The bread fans out for a fun presentation.
—*Kay Daly, Raleigh, NC*

PREP: 10 MIN. • **BAKE:** 25 MIN. • **MAKES:** 8 SERVINGS

1   unsliced round loaf
    sourdough bread (1 lb.)
1   lb. Monterey Jack
    cheese
½   cup butter, melted
½   cup chopped green
    onions
2   to 3 tsp. poppy seeds

1. Preheat oven to 350°. Cut bread widthwise into 1-in.
slices to within ½ in. of bottom of loaf. Repeat cuts in
opposite direction. Cut cheese into ¼-in. slices; cut slices
into small pieces. Place cheese in cuts in bread.

2. In a small bowl, mix butter, green onions and poppy
seeds; drizzle over bread. Wrap in foil; place on a baking
sheet. Bake 15 minutes. Unwrap; bake until cheese is
melted, about 10 minutes longer.

1 SERVING: 481 cal., 31g fat (17g sat. fat), 91mg chol., 782mg
sod., 32g carb. (1g sugars, 2g fiber), 17g pro.

ADVANCE PLANNING
The bread can be sliced and filled a day ahead. Right
before company comes, melt the butter and add the
green onions and poppy seeds.

Fruity Pull-Apart Bread

Who doesn't love to start the day with monkey bread? This
skillet version is packed with bright fresh berries and dolloped with
irresistibly rich cream cheese. A sprinkle of fresh basil brings it all together.
—*Darla Andrews, Schertz, TX*

PREP: 15 MIN. • **BAKE:** 35 MIN. • **MAKES:** 8 SERVINGS

1 tube (16.3 oz.) large
  refrigerated flaky
  honey butter biscuits
½ cup packed dark brown
  sugar
½ cup sugar
⅓ cup butter, melted
1 cup fresh blueberries
1 cup chopped fresh
  strawberries
4 oz. cream cheese,
  softened
1 Tbsp. minced fresh
  basil

1. Preheat oven to 350°. Separate dough into 8 biscuits; cut biscuits into fourths.

2. In a shallow bowl, combine sugars. Dip biscuits in melted butter, then in sugar mixture. Place biscuits in a greased 10¼-in. cast-iron skillet. Top with fresh berries; dollop with cream cheese. Bake until biscuits are golden brown and cooked through, 35-40 minutes. Sprinkle with basil.

1 SERVING: 383 cal., 20g fat (9g sat. fat), 30mg chol., 641mg sod., 49g carb. (28g sugars, 2g fiber), 5g pro.

NOTES

Overnight Cinnamon Rolls

Each one of these soft rolls is packed with cinnamon flavor—they're definitely worth the overnight wait! I like to try different fun fillings, too.
—*Chris O'Connell, San Antonio, TX*

PREP: 35 MIN. + CHILLING • **BAKE:** 20 MIN. • **MAKES:** 2 DOZEN

2 pkg. (¼ oz. each) active dry yeast
1½ cups warm water (110° to 115°)
2 large eggs, room temperature
½ cup butter, softened
½ cup sugar
2 tsp. salt
5¾ to 6¼ cups all-purpose flour

CINNAMON FILLING
1 cup packed brown sugar
4 tsp. ground cinnamon
½ cup softened butter, divided

GLAZE
2 cups confectioners' sugar
¼ cup half-and-half cream
2 tsp. vanilla extract

1. In a small bowl, dissolve yeast in warm water. In a large bowl, combine eggs, butter, sugar, salt, yeast mixture and 3 cups flour; beat on medium speed until smooth. Stir in enough remaining flour to form a very soft dough (dough will be sticky). Do not knead. Cover; refrigerate overnight.

2. In a small bowl, mix brown sugar and cinnamon. Turn dough onto a floured surface; divide dough in half. Roll 1 portion into an 18x12-in. rectangle. Spread with ¼ cup butter to within ½ in. of edges; sprinkle evenly with half of the brown sugar mixture.

3. Roll up jelly-roll style, starting with a long side; pinch seam to seal. Cut into 12 slices. Place slices in a greased 13x9-in. baking pan, cut side down. Repeat with the remaining dough and filling.

4. Cover with kitchen towels; let rise in a warm place until doubled, about 1 hour.

5. Bake at 375° for 20-25 minutes or until lightly browned. For the glaze, mix confectioners' sugar, cream and vanilla; spread over warm rolls.

1 ROLL: 278 cal., 9g fat (5g sat. fat), 39mg chol., 262mg sod., 47g carb. (23g sugars, 1g fiber), 4g pro.

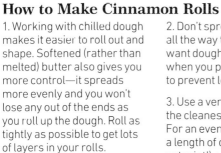

How to Make Cinnamon Rolls

1. Working with chilled dough makes it easier to roll out and shape. Softened (rather than melted) butter also gives you more control—it spreads more evenly and you won't lose any out of the ends as you roll up the dough. Roll as tightly as possible to get lots of layers in your rolls.

2. Don't spread the filling all the way to the edge; you want dough touching dough when you pinch the seam shut to prevent leaks.

3. Use a very sharp knife for the cleanest possible cut. For an even cleaner cut, loop a length of dental floss (plain, not mint!) around the roll and pull it tight to cut your slices.

Garlic Rosemary Pull-Apart Bread

This recipe is a different type of pull-apart bread. Eat it by itself, dipped in marinara, or as part of a meal. For a different flavor, add sun-dried tomatoes, pesto, or an onion soup mix packet instead of the rosemary-garlic combo.
—*Christina Trikoris, Clarksville, TN*

PREP: 25 MIN. + RISING • **BAKE:** 55 MIN. + COOLING • **MAKES:** 16 SERVINGS

3 tsp. active dry yeast

1 tsp. salt

5¼ to 6 cups all-purpose flour

1 cup water

1 cup butter, cubed

½ cup 2% milk

2 large eggs, room temperature

FLAVORING

½ cup butter, melted

6 garlic cloves, minced

2 Tbsp. minced fresh rosemary or 2 tsp. dried rosemary, crushed

1 tsp. salt

1 cup grated Parmesan cheese

1. In a large bowl, mix yeast, salt and 2 cups flour. In a small saucepan, heat water, cubed butter and milk to 120°-130°. Add to dry ingredients; beat on medium speed for 2 minutes. Add eggs; beat on high for 2 minutes. Stir in enough remaining flour to form a soft dough (dough will be sticky).

2. Turn dough onto a floured surface; knead until smooth and elastic, 6-8 minutes. Place in a greased bowl, turning once to grease the top. Cover and let rise in a warm place until doubled, about 1 hour.

3. Punch dough down. Turn onto a lightly floured surface; shape into 1½-in. balls. Combine the melted butter, garlic, rosemary and salt. Dip 10 dough balls into butter mixture. Place in a greased 10-in. fluted tube pan; sprinkle with a scant ¼ cup Parmesan cheese. Repeat with the remaining balls and Parmesan cheese. Drizzle with any remaining butter mixture. Cover and let rise until doubled, about 45 minutes.

4. Bake at 350° until golden brown, 55-70 minutes or until a thermometer inserted into bread reads 200°. Cool in pan for 10 minutes before inverting onto a serving plate. Serve warm.

1 SERVING: 341 cal., 20g fat (12g sat. fat), 74mg chol., 536mg sod., 33g carb. (1g sugars, 1g fiber), 7g pro.

Cinnamon Swirl Bread

Your family will be impressed with the soft texture and appealing swirls of cinnamon in these lovely breakfast loaves.
—Diane Armstrong, Elm Grove, WI

PREP: 25 MIN. + RISING • **BAKE:** 30 MIN. • **MAKES:** 2 LOAVES (16 SLICES EACH)

- 2 **pkg. (¼ oz. each) active dry yeast**
- ⅓ **cup warm water (110° to 115°)**
- 1 **cup warm 2% milk (110° to 115°)**
- 1 **cup sugar, divided**
- 2 **large eggs, room temperature**
- 6 **Tbsp. butter, softened**
- 1½ **tsp. salt**
- 5½ **to 6 cups all-purpose flour**
- 2 **Tbsp. ground cinnamon**

READER REVIEW

"This bread is amazing and fairly easy for this first-timer. My swirl is perfect! The crust is perfect and the taste is perfect! I can't wait to try using it for French toast!"

—ERIN, TASTEOFHOME.COM

1. In a large bowl, dissolve yeast in warm water. Add warm milk, ½ cup sugar, eggs, butter, salt and 3 cups flour; beat on medium speed until smooth. Stir in enough remaining flour to form a soft dough.

2. Turn dough onto a floured surface; knead until smooth and elastic, 6-8 minutes. Place in a greased bowl, turning once to grease the top. Cover; let rise in a warm place until doubled, about 1 hour.

3. Mix cinnamon and the remaining sugar. Punch down dough. Turn onto a lightly floured surface; divide in half. Roll each portion into an 18x8-in. rectangle; sprinkle each with about ¼ cup cinnamon sugar to within ½ in. of edges. Roll up jelly-roll style, starting with a short side; pinch seam to seal. Place in 2 greased 9x5-in. loaf pans, seam side down.

4. Cover with kitchen towels; let rise in a warm place until doubled, about 1½ hours.

5. Bake at 350° until golden brown, 30-35 minutes. Remove from pans to wire racks to cool.

1 SLICE: 132 cal., 3g fat (2g sat. fat), 20mg chol., 141mg sod., 23g carb. (7g sugars, 1g fiber), 3g pro.

Heavenly Cheese Danish

This tempting cheese Danish is baked to flaky perfection and made to shine with a simple egg wash gloss. It tastes just as decadent as any breakfast pastry you'd find in a bakery or coffee shop.
—*Josephine Triton, Lakewood, OH*

PREP: 50 MIN. + CHILLING • **BAKE:** 15 MIN. • **MAKES:** 16 ROLLS

2 pkg. (¼ oz. each) active dry yeast
½ cup warm water (110° to 115°)
4 cups all-purpose flour
⅓ cup sugar
2 tsp. salt
1 cup cold butter, cubed
1 cup 2% milk
4 large egg yolks, room temperature
3 tsp. ground cinnamon, divided

ASSEMBLY
12 oz. cream cheese, softened
⅓ cup sugar
1 large egg, separated, room temperature
1 Tbsp. water
2 Tbsp. maple syrup

1. Dissolve yeast in warm water. In another bowl, mix flour, sugar and salt; cut in butter until crumbly. Add milk, egg yolks and yeast mixture; stir to form a soft dough (dough will be sticky). Cover and refrigerate 8-24 hours.

2. Punch down dough; divide into 4 portions. On a lightly floured surface, pat each portion into a 9x4-in. rectangle; sprinkle each with ¾ tsp. cinnamon. Cut each rectangle lengthwise into four 9x1-in. strips. Twist each strip, then loosely wrap strip around itself to form a coil; tuck end under and pinch to seal. Place coils 3 in. apart on greased baking sheets.

3. Beat cream cheese, sugar and egg yolk until smooth. Press an indentation in the center of each roll; fill with a rounded tablespoon of the cream cheese mixture. Cover; let rise in a warm place until doubled, about 45 minutes.

4. Whisk egg white with water; brush over rolls. Bake at 350° until golden brown, 15-20 minutes. Remove to wire racks; brush with maple syrup. Serve Danish warm. Refrigerate leftovers.

1 ROLL: 359 cal., 21g fat (12g sat. fat), 111mg chol., 468mg sod., 37g carb. (12g sugars, 1g fiber), 7g pro.

Cinnamon-Walnut Sticky Buns

The sweet honey-walnut topping and tender texture
make these sticky rolls a surefire crowd-pleaser.
—Debbie Broeker, Rocky Mount, MO

PREP: 1 HOUR + RISING • **BAKE:** 30 MIN. • **MAKES:** 2 DOZEN

- 2 **pkg. (¼ oz. each) active dry yeast**
- 1½ **cups warm water (110° to 115°)**
- 1 **cup mashed potatoes (without added milk and butter)**
- ½ **cup sugar**
- ½ **cup butter, softened**
- 2 **large eggs, room temperature**
- 2 **tsp. salt**
- 6 **to 6½ cups all-purpose flour**

TOPPING
- ¼ **cup butter**
- 1 **cup packed brown sugar**
- 1 **cup honey**
- 1 **tsp. ground cinnamon**
- 1 **cup chopped walnuts**

FILLING
- ½ **cup sugar**
- 2 **tsp. ground cinnamon**
- 2 **Tbsp. butter, melted**

1. In a small bowl, dissolve yeast in warm water. In a large bowl, combine mashed potatoes, sugar, butter, eggs, salt, yeast mixture and 2 cups flour; beat on medium speed until smooth. Stir in enough remaining flour to form a soft dough.

2. Turn dough onto a floured surface; knead until smooth and elastic, 6-8 minutes. Place in a greased bowl, turning once to grease the top. Cover and let rise in a warm place until doubled, about 1 hour.

3. For topping, in a small saucepan, melt butter. Stir in brown sugar, honey and cinnamon. Divide mixture among 3 greased 9-in. round baking pans, spreading evenly. Sprinkle with walnuts.

4. For filling, in a small bowl, mix sugar and cinnamon. Punch down dough. Turn onto a lightly floured surface; divide in half. Roll 1 portion into an 18x12-in. rectangle. Brush with 1 Tbsp. melted butter to within ½ in. of edges; sprinkle with ¼ cup sugar mixture.

5. Roll up jelly-roll style, starting with a long side; pinch seam to seal. Cut into 12 slices. Repeat with the remaining dough, butter and sugar mixture. Place 8 slices in each pan, cut side down. Cover with kitchen towels; let rise until doubled, about 30 minutes.

6. Bake at 350° for 30-35 minutes or until golden brown. Immediately invert onto serving plates. Serve warm.

1 BUN: 328 cal., 10g fat (5g sat. fat), 35mg chol., 257mg sod., 55g carb. (29g sugars, 2g fiber), 5g pro.

Traditional New Orleans King Cake

Get in on the fun of king cake, a can't-miss part of Mardi Gras celebrations in New Orleans. Hide a little toy baby in the cake; whoever finds it has one year of good luck!
—Rebecca Baird, Salt Lake City, UT

PREP: 40 MIN. + RISING • **BAKE:** 25 MIN. + COOLING • **MAKES:** 1 CAKE (12 SLICES)

2 pkg. (¼ oz. each) active dry yeast
½ cup warm water (110° to 115°)
¾ cup sugar, divided
½ cup butter, softened
½ cup warm 2% milk (110° to 115°)
2 large egg yolks, room temperature
1¼ tsp. salt
1 tsp. grated lemon zest
¼ tsp. ground nutmeg
3¼ to 3¾ cups all-purpose flour
1 tsp. ground cinnamon
1 large egg, beaten

GLAZE
1½ cups confectioners' sugar
2 tsp. lemon juice
2 to 3 Tbsp. water
Green, purple and yellow sugars

1. In a large bowl, dissolve yeast in warm water. Add ½ cup sugar, the butter, milk, egg yolks, salt, lemon zest, nutmeg and 2 cups of the flour. Beat until smooth. Stir in enough remaining flour to form a soft dough (dough will be sticky).

2. Turn dough onto a floured surface; knead until smooth and elastic, 6-8 minutes. Place in a greased bowl, turning once to grease the top. Cover and let rise in a warm place until doubled, about 1 hour.

3. Punch dough down. Turn onto a lightly floured surface. Roll into a 16x10-in. rectangle. Combine cinnamon and remaining sugar; sprinkle over dough to within ½ in. of edges. Roll up jelly-roll style, starting with a long side; pinch seam to seal. Place seam side down on a greased baking sheet; pinch ends together to form a ring. Cover and let rise until doubled, about 1 hour.

4. Brush ring with egg. Bake at 375° for 25-30 minutes or until golden brown. Cool on a wire rack.

5. For glaze, combine the confectioners' sugar, lemon juice and enough water to achieve desired consistency. Spread over completely cool cake. Sprinkle with colored sugars.

1 SLICE: 321 cal., 9g fat (5g sat. fat), 73mg chol., 313mg sod., 55g carb. (28g sugars, 1g fiber), 5g pro.

Pumpkin-Filled Crescent Rolls

This is an Old World recipe derived from my grandmother, who didn't use traditional measuring cups. We figured out this recipe, which must date back to 1900 or earlier. Other fillings that work well are cranberry, peanut butter or lemon.
—*Gary Wanosky, North Ridgeville, OH*

PREP: 40 MIN. + CHILLING • **BAKE:** 15 MIN./BATCH • **MAKES:** 3 DOZEN

4 tsp. active dry yeast
¼ cup warm 2% milk
   (110° to 115°)
4 cups all-purpose flour
¼ cup sugar
1 tsp. salt
1 cup butter, cubed
½ cup shortening
1 cup sour cream
4 large egg yolks,
   room temperature
2 tsp. grated lemon zest

FILLING
¾ cup canned pumpkin
⅓ cup sugar
1½ tsp. pumpkin pie spice

1. In a small bowl, dissolve yeast in milk. In a large bowl, combine 3 cups flour, sugar and salt; cut in butter and shortening until crumbly. Add the sour cream, egg yolks, lemon zest and yeast mixture; mix well. Stir in enough remaining flour to form a soft dough.

2. Turn dough onto a floured surface; knead until smooth and elastic, 6-8 minutes. Place in a greased bowl, turning once to grease the top. Cover and refrigerate overnight.

3. Let dough stand at room temperature for 1 hour. Punch dough down; turn onto a lightly floured surface. Divide into thirds. Roll each into a 12-in. circle; cut each circle into 12 wedges.

4. Combine filling ingredients; spread a rounded teaspoon of filling over each wedge. Roll up wedges from the wide ends; place point side down 2 in. apart on greased baking sheets. Curve ends to form crescents. Cover and let rise in a warm place for 30 minutes.

5. Preheat oven to 350°. Bake crescents until golden brown, 13-18 minutes. Remove from pans to wire racks.

1 ROLL: 156 cal., 10g fat (5g sat. fat), 41mg chol., 106mg sod., 15g carb. (4g sugars, 1g fiber), 2g pro.

Chocolate & Cherry Stromboli

This melty, chocolaty spin on stromboli is delicious for both breakfast and dessert.
Serve it with a cup of coffee, and even the coldest winter day instantly feels more snug.
—Lorraine Caland, Shuniah, ON

PREP: 40 MIN. + RISING • **BAKE:** 20 MIN. + COOLING • **MAKES:** 1 LOAF (12 SLICES)

4 cups all-purpose flour
1 pkg. (¼ oz.) quick-rise yeast
1 tsp. salt
1 cup warm water (120° to 130°)
3 Tbsp. canola oil
2 Tbsp. honey
1 large egg, room temperature, lightly beaten
1 tsp. lemon juice
8 oz. finely chopped bittersweet chocolate, divided
½ cup dried cherries, chopped
2 Tbsp. coarse sugar

MAKE IT YOUR OWN
For contrast, drizzle a light glaze of bright white icing over the dark chocolate. Almost any dried fruit would be great in this; try apricots, dried plums or dried cranberries.

1. In a large bowl, whisk 3 cups flour, yeast and salt. In another bowl, mix water, oil and honey. Add to the dry ingredients; beat on medium speed for 2 minutes. Stir in enough remaining flour to form a soft dough (dough will be sticky).

2. Turn dough onto a floured surface; knead until smooth and elastic, 3-5 minutes. Place in a greased bowl, turning once to grease top. Cover; let rise in a warm place until doubled, about 30 minutes.

3. Preheat oven to 400°. Press dough into a greased 15x10x1-in. baking pan. Whisk egg with lemon juice; brush dough with half of egg wash. Sprinkle half the chocolate evenly over dough; top with cherries. Fold long sides of dough over chocolate and cherries, overlapping the edges, and leaving the ends open. Brush with the remaining egg wash. Sprinkle with coarse sugar. Bake on lowest oven rack until bread sounds hollow when tapped, about 20 minutes. Cool on wire rack.

4. In a microwave, melt the remaining chocolate. Drizzle over the cooled bread.

1 SLICE: 248 cal., 8g fat (2g sat. fat), 16mg chol., 205mg sod., 36g carb. (10g sugars, 2g fiber), 5g pro.

Caramel-Pecan Monkey Bread

The kids will get a kick out of pulling off gooey pieces of this delectable monkey bread. It's hard to resist the caramel-coated treat.
—Taste of Home *Test Kitchen*

PREP: 20 MIN. + CHILLING • **BAKE:** 30 MIN. + COOLING • **MAKES:** 20 SERVINGS

1 pkg. (¼ oz.) active dry yeast
¼ cup warm water (110° to 115°)
5 Tbsp. plus ½ cup butter, divided
1¼ cups warm 2% milk (110° to 115°)
2 large eggs, room temperature
1¼ cups sugar, divided
1 tsp. salt
5 cups all-purpose flour
1 tsp. ground cinnamon

CARAMEL
⅔ cup packed brown sugar
¼ cup butter, cubed
¼ cup heavy whipping cream
¾ cup chopped pecans, divided

GLAZE (OPTIONAL)
4 oz. cream cheese, softened
¼ cup butter, softened
1½ cups confectioners' sugar
3 to 5 Tbsp. 2% milk

1. Dissolve yeast in warm water. Melt 5 Tbsp. butter. Add milk, eggs and melted butter to yeast mixture; stir in ¼ cup sugar, salt and 3 cups flour. Beat on medium speed for 3 minutes. Stir in enough remaining flour to form a firm dough.

2. Turn onto a floured surface; knead until smooth and elastic, 6-8 minutes. Place in a greased bowl, turning once to grease the top. Refrigerate, covered, overnight.

3. Punch dough down; shape into 40 balls (about 1¼ in. diameter). Melt the remaining ½ cup butter; pour into a shallow bowl. In a second shallow bowl, combine cinnamon and the remaining sugar. Dip balls in butter, then roll in sugar mixture.

4. For caramel, bring brown sugar, butter and cream to a boil in a small saucepan over medium heat. Cook and stir for 3 minutes. Pour half of the caramel into a greased 10-in. fluted tube pan; layer with half the pecans and half the dough balls; repeat. Cover and let rise until doubled, about 45 minutes.

5. Bake at 350° until golden brown, 30-40 minutes. (Cover loosely with foil for last 10 minutes if the top browns too quickly.) Cool in pan for 10 minutes before inverting onto a serving plate.

6. For glaze, beat cream cheese and butter until blended; gradually beat in confectioners' sugar. Add enough milk to reach desired consistency. Drizzle glaze over warm bread.

2 PIECES: 334 cal., 15g fat (8g sat. fat), 52mg chol., 207mg sod., 45g carb. (21g sugars, 1g fiber), 5g pro.

Recipe Index